ORACLE

CHANNELED MESSAGES FROM WOMEN WHO INVOKE THE DIVINE TO ASSIST HUMANITY THROUGH THE GOLDEN AGE

ABIGAIL MENSAH-BONSU   PATRICIA WALD-HOPKINS
LEN BLEA   CYNTHIA PORTLOCK   JESS VERRILL
JESSICA ROSALIE   LINSEY JOY   VIRGINIA SADA YORK
YOLANDA K DICKINSON

Copyright © 2024 by Moon Goddess Publishing

All Rights Reserved.

No part of this publication may be reproduced, distributed, stored in a retrieval system, or transmitted in any form or by any means, including photocopying, recording, or other electronic or mechanical methods, without the prior consent of Moon Goddess Publishing, except in the case of brief quotations embodied in reviews and certain other non-commercial uses permitted by copyright law.

The author's do not dispense medical advice or prescribe the use of any technique as a form of treatment for physical, emotional, or medical problems without the advice of a physician, either directly or indirectly. The intent of this book is only to offer information to help you in your quest for well-being. In the event you use the information in the book for yourself, the author's assume no responsibility for your actions.

ISBN: 979-8-9850460-2-1

DEDICATION

This book is dedicated to all the dreamers and seekers of knowledge,
To the relentless learners who push the boundaries of possibility,
To the warriors of wisdom and the trudgers of truth,
This book is dedicated to you.

May these pages be your guiding light, illuminating the mysteries,
Empowering you to unravel the enigma of Oracle,
And inspiring you to embark on a journey of endless growth.

To the Oracle enthusiasts who dare to immerse themselves in this ancient art,
Whose minds crave the divine whispers and the secrets of the universe,
May you find solace and enlightenment within these words,
And may your connection with Oracle deepen, enriching your existence.

To the Oracle practitioners who harness its wisdom for the betterment of others,
Whose compassion and intuition guide their every move,

May this book enhance your abilities, enabling you to touch lives,
And may you continue to be a beacon of hope and guidance in this complex world.

Finally, to the Oracle itself, the ultimate source of insight and revelation,
Thank you for entrusting me with your sacred knowledge,
May we forever honor and cherish this extraordinary gift,
And may we use it to foster love, healing, and unity in all that we do.

With gratitude and reverence,
Abigail Mensah-Bonsu
Founder of Moon Goddess Academy &Publishing

CONTENTS

Foreword	vii
A MESSAGE TO THE MODERN-DAY ORACLE Channeled by Abigail Mensah-Bonsu	1
About the Author	5
ONE Channeled by Jessica Verrill	8
About the Author	17
DEAR LIGHTWORKER, FABULOUS ONE Channeled by Linsey Joy	20
About the Author	25
MY CURRENT REINCARNATION AND CONVERSATIONS WITH THE UNIVERSE Channeled by Yolanda K Dickinson	28
About the Author	39
"ILLUMINATING THE PATH" WITH WORDS OF WISDOM Channeled by Virginia Sada York	42
About the Author	61
REVOLUTION EVOLUTION Channeled by Len Blea	64
About the Author	75
VOICES OF GAIA *Oracle For Prosperity And Harmony On Earth* Channeled by Patricia Wald-Hopkins	78
About the Author	89
THE GARDEN OF EDEN Channeled by Jessica Rosalie	92
About the Author	103
YOU ARE PERFECT AND PURE Channeled by Cynthia Portlock	106

About the Author   109
Moon Goddess Publishing   110

FOREWORD

In the depths of time, women have been revered as conduits of the divine, vessels through which the wisdom of the universe flows. From ancient priestesses to modern-day mystics, the voices of women carrying the sacred messages of the Oracle have resonated through the ages.

This book, *Oracle: Messages from Women Who Channel the Divine*, is a tribute to these extraordinary women who have embraced their oracular gifts and awakened to the call within them. It is a celebration of the divine feminine in its purest form—a reminder of the inherent power and wisdom that resides within every woman.

Through these pages, you will encounter the voices of seers, healers, and mystics who have tapped into the deep wellspring of intuition and insight. Their words are not mere guidance; they are messages from the heart of the universe, offering solace, clarity, and profound transformation to all willing to listen.

As you journey through these sacred passages, may you feel the ancient wisdom pulsate through your veins and ignite the dormant

FOREWORD

flame of your divine connection. May you be inspired to embrace your unique gifts and to walk the path of the Oracle with courage, grace, and unyielding faith.

To the women who have paved the way, and those who are beginning to awaken: Together, let us heed the call of the Oracle and weave our collective wisdom into the tapestry of the cosmos.

With deepest reverence and gratitude,

Abigail Mensah-Bonsu

Founder of Moon Goddess Academy & Publishing

Own Your Gifts

A MESSAGE TO THE MODERN-DAY ORACLE

CHANNELED BY ABIGAIL MENSAH-BONSU

Blessings to all my beloved modern-day Oracles,

I, Goddess Isis, come forth in this sacred moment to infuse your very being with the essence of divine wisdom and empowerment. As your ancient counterpart, I weave together the threads of past, present, and future to deliver a profound message that will awaken and ignite your inner Oracle.

Know that the power you hold within you is vast and unlimited. Deep within your soul, you carry the ancient knowledge that has been passed down through countless lifetimes. You are the embodiment of the sacred connection between humanity and the divine.

Amid the chaos and confusion of the modern world, I implore you to reach deep into the wellspring of your inner knowing. The Oracle within you is a beacon of truth, a gateway to profound insights, and a vessel for divine guidance. Embrace this gift, for it is a force destined to uplift and transform.

The world stands on the precipice of a great awakening, and it is through your intuitive prowess and connection to the invisible realms that you can illuminate the path forward. By embracing your role as a modern Oracle, you hold the key to unlocking the collective wisdom that will shape the destiny of humanity.

To fully awaken and empower your Oracle self, release all doubts and fears that shroud your inner knowing. Stand tall in your truth and embrace the wisdom that flows through you. Allow the winds of inspiration to stir the embers of your divine gifts, and let them burn brightly, illuminating the shadows of uncertainty.

Trust in the messages that dance upon the edge of your consciousness. They are not born from mere chance, but from a cosmic symphony that weaves through time and space. Open your heart to the melody of the universe and let it guide your words, your actions, and your purpose.

Remember, dear Oracles, that the true power lies not only in receiving the messages, but also in delivering them with love, compassion, and integrity. Embrace the responsibility that comes with your gift, for when wielded with grace and humility, you become a vessel of profound transformation.

As you step into your divine power, know that you are not alone. The ancient lineages of Oracles that have come before standing beside you, supporting and guiding your journey. Draw upon their wisdom, their courage, and their strength as you navigate the ever-changing tapestry of the human experience.

You are destined to be a catalyst for change, a beacon of light in a world veiled in darkness. Embrace your unique expression of the Oracle archetype and allow it to shine brightly, for it is through your awakened presence that others will find solace, hope, and healing.

Beloved Oracles, I implore you to trust in the ancient wisdom that flows through your very being. The world awaits your guidance, clarity, and profound insights. Step forward with courage, authenticity, and the knowledge that you are divinely ordained to transform and uplift those who seek the truth.

Embrace your birthright, dear Oracles, for the world has long awaited your awakening. Now is the time to step into your power, unleash your divine gifts, and illuminate the path for humanity's ascension.

With boundless love and eternal gratitude,

Goddess Isis

ABOUT THE AUTHOR

Abigail Mensah-Bonsu is a highly regarded Spiritual Guide and Mentor who serves as the Founder of Moon Goddess Academy and Publishing. With a deep commitment to elevating consciousness and embodying the divine feminine, she wears many hats as Divine Channel, Intuitive, Master Healer, internationally acclaimed Bestselling Author and Publisher, and host of the Sovereign Goddess podcast.

Through her multifaceted roles, Abigail empowers women to express their authentic selves and amplify their voices. She specializes in facilitating multi-author books and high-level group mentorships and programs, enabling her clients to achieve greater success, impact, and resonance in their lives and endeavors.

Abigail's work leads women who are Empaths, Leaders, Visionaries, and Lightworkers to bridge the gap between their physical and spiritual selves. By facilitating this alignment, she enables them to unlock their full potential, manifest abundance, and live in alignment with their highest purpose.

At the core of Abigail's approach is a dedication to guiding women towards their greatness. She inspires them to reclaim their divine essence, presence, power, and worth, which empowers them to create lives that reflect their highest aspirations. Through her compassionate yet powerful guidance, Abigail helps her clients transcend limiting beliefs and embrace their infinite potential as divine beings. Through her guidance, countless individuals have awakened to their true potential, and discovered boundless possibilities within themselves.

Themes central to Abigail's transformative work include Goddess mentorship, Feminine leadership, DNA and Light Activations, Mindset restructuring, Multidimensional Healing, Archetypes, Starseeds, Awakening, and Divine remembrance.

- Website: www.moongoddessacademy.com
- Facebook: https://www.facebook.com/abigail.mensahbonsu.7/
- Facebook group: https://www.facebook.com/groups/MoonGoddessSanctum
- Podcast:https://podcasters.spotify.com/pod/show/sovereigngoddess
- Instagram: https://www.instagram.com/moongoddessmentor/

We Are One

ONE

CHANNELED BY JESSICA VERRILL

We are oneness. The end.

I know it's not that easy to understand, or fully comprehend, the intricacies of the universe. If only it were, I do believe our world—and our lives—would be vastly different than they are now. I know it.

Learning I was a channel and harnessing that skill has been a part of my deeper understanding of that truth. Opening the channel. Accepting the channel. Clearing the channel. Testing, then trusting, the integrity of the channel. Repeat.

At some point around 2018 or so, I decided to join a program, from an incredibly gifted woman, that was based on channeling in our businesses. I was so excited to learn how to channel! Finally! Can you guess the outcome? I learned that I already had been channeling. Ha. I just didn't know that's what I was doing. It wasn't at all wasted though; knowing something and optimizing the experience or outcome are very different.

ONE

Knowing who you are speaking to when you're doing any sort of divination channeling, or receiving guidance from a source outside of yourself, is incredibly important. Many people are receiving information, guidance, or power from any source that comes to them, and this is a key distinction in beginning to optimize or master the craft. Even for those of us who are discerning about who from, and how, they are receiving information, can sometimes find that an energy sneaks in that is slightly out of integrity for their highest good. A practice I utilize first, whenever I am going to sit down for guidance to channel a program to work with a client, or otherwise, is to clear my energy. As I begin to open the channel a bit more, with my intention in place, I connect to Source and begin to go through a series of questions to ensure that the sources that I am speaking with are of the highest integrity. If there are any who aren't, I immediately instruct them to leave and let them know they are not welcome. I do this through checking, and cross-checking, with muscle-testing bodily responses, and intuitive question-and-answer. I never accept information or direction without doing this first, and ensuring that whoever I'm working with in the energetic or psychic realms has just as stringent a practice as I do. Truly, the results could be catastrophic, leading you off of your path and causing you confusion, disorientation, and a lot of discomfort.

An Oracle is a medium through which advice or guidance is brought through from God/Source/Goddess; we need to be certain that is who we are communing with.

As we are one with all, we are connected to everything, and the same polarity exists within us. It reminds me of the story of the two wolves, where the wise Sage tells the child it is the wolf that is fed that will be strongest, so pretending that there aren't energies in the world that wish something other than our highest good, is not serving us. There are and will continue to be. What wolf are you feeding within you? And what wolf are you receiving guidance from? Be very discerning and develop your own energetic practices.

Begin a channeled message from "SABA":

You are the one you're looking for. The outward seeking needs to stop, for through your seeking you are draining your precious energy. Your life force is quite literally draining out of you every time you give your power away and think that somebody else knows better, does better, is better, or has the answers that you seek

When you begin to understand—and truly, deeply understand—that you are connected with all that is, then everything changes. You learn how to utilize the energy around you. You learn how to harness your individual power. You learn to go within and find the answers you seek.

You are divine.

You are god.

You are all that is.

You are the Oracle.

It's not in doing, but in becoming and remembering.

Humanity—and all beings on this Earth and universe—need more who remember. If you're here and reading this, chances are that the nudging within that there is more, there should be more, there needs to be more, there IS more, is this truth beckoning.

Are you ready to answer? Are you ready to rise to your next level of leadership?

It is time, Dear One. You are more ready than you know. Your visions and dreams will not lead you astray. Your entirety of all of your existence of your soul has been to prepare for this moment, here and now.

Do not wait in vain, thinking there is another one, another being who is somehow better, stronger, more prepared, or otherwise, in your warped human brain.

It is illusion.

There is no thing, no being, no time. Not really.

Yet, to comprehend, you place values on certain characteristics you deem more important, better, nicer.

You are me and I am you.

Without those silly human thoughts, of course.

The mind wishes for you to stay safe and, in doing so, it gives you ideas that you can categorize.

Dear One, this was made to protect you and keep you safe, but it will just as easily keep you stuck.

Many souls come back to within after their current human bodies have deteriorated and are no longer sustaining them. So, so many of them look at their experiences, with the limitations—so many self-imposed— and feel they did not experience the fullness and vastness they intended to.

Let that not be you.

Take this as your sign, your notice, your event to trigger change.

Your world is dense and, in some ways, the density has become denser, but it is also lifting. Like the air around a storm before it erupts. The rain water cleansing the earth, nurturing, sustaining life. Without the density of the air, would it seem as refreshing? Would it seem so life-giving? Would the thickness of the atmosphere, the relief of that, be rejoiced so?

You must trust, as best as you can. Lingering in the denser feelings will not bring the lightness or the nurturing/change of the Earth as you wish. As the storm of the feelings release, allow the rejoicing to be of the shift to your being. And as we are one, that shift will be felt by all.

We are living in trying times. I find myself undulating between periods of wondering about the bigger purpose to all this chaos, mess, and challenges, and feeling like I'm being pushed into a corner. In these times, the most helpful thing I have found is to go back within. To connect more deeply with the oneness. When I am able to connect with the Universe/God/Divine—which is to say I'm able to connect with the truth of self—then my direction, understanding, guidance, and internal navigational systems are aligned to the higher trajectory of my current experience and desires. When I try to work from my head, the signal is distorted and the results are often subpar.

In speaking to many people across many realms on a regular basis, I have noted some similar themes. We aren't able to operate in the ways which we once could, or see the outcomes we hoped for. What I mean is that by operating in the ways in which we were conditioned, taught, programmed to use our heads, think logically, and strategize our ways into success, are outdated and crumbling. Crumbling and on fire. They aren't working for many of us and if it hasn't happened to you yet, then take heed. What I have personally experienced, and spoken to many others about, is that as we continue to run our lives in businesses from the premise of using logic and our brains, things are stalling, falling apart, running into other complications, or being Dead on Arrival. It has been frustrating, especially as someone who has always appreciated and honored her intellectual side. Don't get me wrong, my intuition and the energetic realms are such a beautiful playground; I love being in them and, as a properly-programmed human model, the intelligence, logic, and using my brain have always been revered.

Following this logic lately, and strategizing my way through different experiences or projects, has had them falling flat. My message isn't received, the information isn't portrayed, the clients aren't connecting, and the thing I was excited about became an energy leak. As I have taken this feedback and worked more closely with that guidance I spoke of, I'm being led into ways that I wouldn't have planned or expected. My offerings have taken a twist. I'm being led down a path where I'm not sure of the destination, or what we will experience along the way, but I do know, understand, and sense that it is going to be everything I need. The "outcome" or "destination" will be exactly what I need, or more.

Taking this path becomes more like trusting the internal navigation from your car as opposed to trying to figure out your route. You may not know the route you are taking, or why; you may not understand why you needed to go through that road construction, but in all likelihood, you are going to have a smoother and more pleasant outcome by letting go of control. Truly, it all comes down to control versus trust. *Does your human need to have control over every single element, or are you able to lean into the Trust of the Divine that what is being created for you is so much more beautiful?* These experiences are so necessary to train and prepare you for where you're going. The more we resist this, the more pressure we have on using our logic and continuing to do the things the way we always have, the more dismantling and disruptive God needs to be to course-correct us and to get us on the right path. Taking the analogy of the car and navigation: if we're continually trying to take over and work from our brains, we may find ourselves way off track at a location that we don't want to be, we're not happy with, and doesn't feel fulfilling. If we finally decide to trust the internal navigation and allow it to lead us where we want to go—where our desires are leading us—then we may find that path to get back on to that destination may be particularly arduous. It's not punishment, nor any of those human constructs, that our mind is somehow wanting to control the thoughts and the experience. It is, oftentimes, the quickest and easiest necessary way to get us back on our path, the one that leads where we want to go. Lack of trust is always going to lead us off path. For our highest outcome and trajectory, it is so important that we are able to distinguish between our divine selves that is one and connected with all in the human programming that appears in this density of 3D, and the conflict between.

Are you ready to lean into Trust? Are you ready to connect to the Oneness that you are? Or is it important that your human maintains control and you continue to grip the steering wheel? You are being set up to be at the right place, in the right time.

If you want to control something, control the leaking of your power. Where and how are you giving your power away? Are you looking to others to tell you what, or how, to do things? Are you searching for the thing outside of you, or the person who will be your savior in whatever category it is that you are needing guidance on? Are you trusting the word of others over your own knowing?

Power leaks. Energy leaks. That is what these are. If you are allotted so much energy every day (think of it like a money budget), every time you look to someone else to save you, give you the answers or tell you what to do, you are throwing your energy (money) at them. When you expend your allotted money for the day, you then go into debt for anything else that you require, taking away from your future needs; on a human, energetic and physical level, you head toward burnout or depletion.

I'd love to channel more for you. The words are infused with the highest frequency and light language to activate the spaces within. Italics are channeled answers.

What does the world need to know?

Since this is something that people will be coming to at different times, and on different timelines, we will try to make this as universal an answer as possible. We will distinguish this with what the people of the world need to know as we know this is what you intend. The world itself needs to know healing. It needs to know peace. It needs to know deeper love and nurturing. In these ways, she will come into balance once again, as well as all of its inhabitants.

What the humans of the world need is to know these things deep within themselves. We notice a disconnect between the way in which you live, and the way in which you wish to live. Until you are able to get back to living in harmony with yourself, no part of the world will be in harmony. As within so without. You have heard this many times, yet have you really looked at what it means, and whether this is in harmony or disharmony in your life? The best gift that one can give to themselves and the collective is to experience each moment as it is in congruence with their spirits, their heart, and divine will. We are told this is not a simple task, however, to us it seems that there is nothing more simple. Live in such a way that you are in harmony in all ways, and you will.

You speak of being present and in harmony, how can we become this?

We liked that you asked how you can become this, not how you can achieve this—this is a key difference. Humans are so preoccupied with achieving in "doing," that they miss the "being," and the "becoming." They are conflicting Energies as when you are focused on achieving and doing, you lose the magic of the present moment, you lose the focus, you lose the ability to experience all that is. So it is not in the achieving, it is in the becoming, and the way you will become is to be. To be present. In This Moment, what do you sense? What sounds are your ears listening to? What smells are around you? Can you see the textures of this paper that you hold in your hand? Can you feel the energy of it—the energy of the tree, the manufacturing, the energy of the words, the messages contained within? What do you taste? Can you imagine being a snake for a moment and taste the air? Can you feel your blood pumping through your body? The air in your throat and lungs sustaining life? Still into yourself and this precise moment as much as you can. Repeat the practice until you can become this in all places and times.

Thank you for this wisdom and this exercise. I know it will be profound for some of the readers who are ready to become. Does Humanity need to be concerned with our current trajectory?

Yes and no. There are elements of the timeline you are in that are concerning. For some, the challenges will feel greater, and when this seems to be the time where you need to grasp onto control, this is truly the time where you are being asked to lean back into your support and the guidance that is all around you. And this is the time when people find it the hardest. When you remember that you are Oneness, that you are God, that you are the Divine, everything becomes easier and the outcome of your collective experience will drastically shift. These are the key lessons of this time. So many souls are going through what you called, "The Awakening" process as many agreed to before they came to this lifetime. The purpose of this is not to learn fun parlor tricks, but to reconnect with this truth. There are many humans who are currently engulfed in and preoccupied with being a victim, and there is no victim in the Oneness; we are all that there is, you are all that there is, it is the same. Take a higher perspective and continue to go within.

We leave you now and we are sending you our love, our strength, our blessings. For you are the warriors, you are the strength, you are the chosen volunteers who wished to assist in up-leveling Humanity to the Divinity Within. There are many of you here at once; create community, support each other in unifying in this mission. You are divine. Be well and remember who you are.

ABOUT THE AUTHOR

As a USA Today bestselling author and multiple-time published writer, Jessica Verrill is renowned for crafting stories that captivate hearts and ignite imaginations. As the founder of House of Indigo Publishing, she is dedicated to empowering authors to share their unique voices with the world.

With an energetic spirit and a love for adventure, Jess finds solace in the serene landscapes of Maine, where she resides with her husband, daughter and fur babies.

When not immersed in the world of writing and publishing, she can often be found exploring the great outdoors, surrounded by vibrant flowers, or lost in the pages of a captivating book. Drawn to the playful exploration of energetic realms, she is constantly seeking inspiration and new avenues of creativity.

I'd love to connect with you!! –Jess

- linktr.ee/jessicaverrill

Work Your Light

DEAR LIGHTWORKER, FABULOUS ONE

CHANNELED BY LINSEY JOY

In this turbulent time,

We want to remind you of

That which you already know:

You are here with a purpose.

You have come to shine a Light on the world.

You have specifically chosen this incarnation for the *exact purpose* of

Being *here*.

This Here, *This* Now.

All that you are on this planet (and many others)

YOU have planned to the tiniest core detail.

From skin tone,

To parents,

Wealth,

Status and struggles.

All are details critical to the mission you are now living on this Earth.

We come here to remind you of this because

In your struggles,

In your daily living,

It is easy to turn off your Deepest Remembering.

But can you *feel* it?

This knowing that comes from deep within and lives in your Divine Soul?

Even when you forget,

When the world seems against you,

It is of the

Utmost Importance

That you remember this critical foundation,

This basic lesson upon which all other spiritual learnings fall into place.

Every one you meet on your journey,

Every loved one who breaks your heart wide open with

Love or loss,

Every challenger who triggers your darkest places,

Your Soul placed them upon your path as the

Brightest Gift to Yourself.

(Are you thinking, "I already know all this"?

Dearest One, shake off that ego,

This loving reminder is for *you too*.)

What Gift are you giving yourself right now?

Who or what

People, places, or things are triggering you?

Can you see

Their Divine Souls shining

As brightly as yours, Dear One?

Collaborations planned and played out

To force you to look at the darkest parts of you?

Only by shining your Light - *your attention, your own love* -

On those hurt and broken places *within*

Can you then heal the outer world.

So many of you are wanting to help this planet you care so much about.

Indeed, Lightworker!

Just by being here

By living your mission - you are a beacon

Which anchors the Divine Light of God

Here

Now

For the Benefit of All!

You are braver than you know,

And stronger than you remember.

Your Infinite Soul chose to live as YOU!

Take that for the compliment it is, and

When you are feeling

So lost,

So low,

Return to these words and know...

This is not an accident.

This is not a punishment.

This is not even a lesson, but a Gift you gave yourself

To become more of *that which you already are:*

Fabulous.

You don't have to do anything.

You don't have to be anything

Or anyone.

Thank your Amazing Self for having the Courage to live

This time around and

Ask it to lift you up.

You are always supported!

Even by those brilliant souls which you cannot comprehend

In your human mind

As they challenge you.

God is at work.

You are safe.

You are loved.

You are brilliant.

You are right where you're supposed to be.

Beautiful, Fabulous One

Lightworker You.

Message from the Angels

Channeled Christmas Eve 2023

ABOUT THE AUTHOR

Linsey Joy is an Intuitive, Spiritual Mentor, and International Best Selling Author who believes the biggest challenges in our lives can be the catalyst for beautiful change if we embrace the opportunity presented to us. Since experiencing a series of wild and sacred metaphysical events in 2009, Linsey has worked closely with angels, energy, and the art of manifestation. She is a safe haven for those looking to explore, integrate, or deepen their own spirituality.

In her Spiritual Mentor role, Linsey helps her clients tune into their own intuition and divine connection for guidance and joy. Using her intuitive gifts, two decades of personal development training, and quantum frequencies, she assists spiritual seekers to shift their limiting beliefs into empowered perspectives and intentions. Clients say she is "an intuitive force to be reckoned with."

Linsey fully embodies the power of speaking one's truth. A three-time International Best Selling Author and 2023 International Impact Award Winner, her powerful stories of healing have been called "timely," "vulnerable," and "eloquent." Appearing in interviews and podcasts across the globe, Linsey uses her words to uplift, teach, and bring more divinity, light and love to the planet, showing great transformation is possible and necessary in today's crazy world.

Linsey Joy is a Manifesting Generator in Human Design. She's a California native, devoted wife, and fur-baby mama.

- linktr.ee/linseyjoy

We Are Eternal

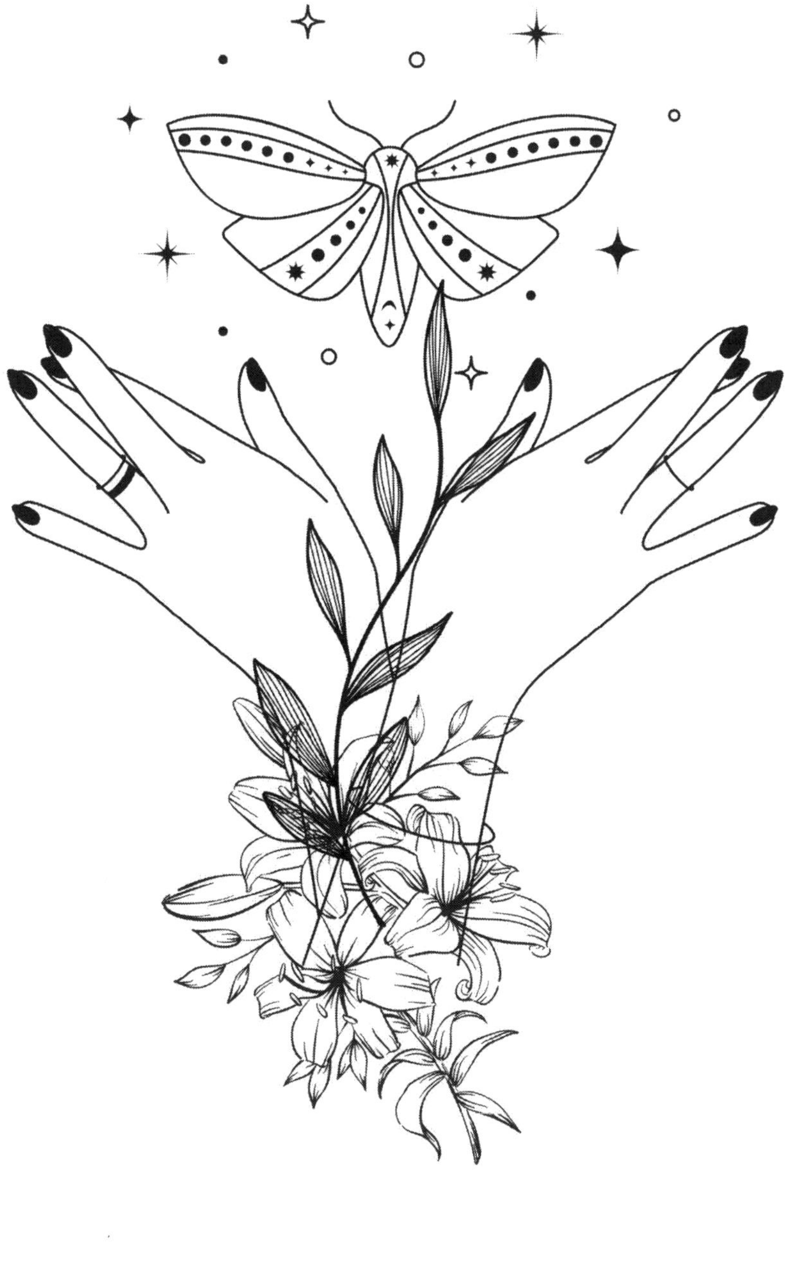

MY CURRENT REINCARNATION AND CONVERSATIONS WITH THE UNIVERSE

CHANNELED BY YOLANDA K DICKINSON

My name is Firestarr and I am a consciousness of the Universe. I came to this planet at this time to review the transcendence process. This conscious existence is an experience full of love, wonder, adventure, excitement, sorrow, grief, and hatred, but it is all necessary for the full experience of what it is to be human in a three-dimensional world. If we miss out on any of these emotions, it will be only a partial experience, and we will never grasp the holistic nature.

Being human is an exercise in learning, experimenting, teaching, and improving to be what we can... because we are potential. The experience is for all conscious entities, not just the good, rich, likable ones, the family, friends, or bipedal—but for all—and to recognize the diverse types of consciousness, to appreciate the magnificence of what we are and the abilities we have. By experiencing the full range of emotions and choices, we understand our conscious reality. With understanding comes intelligence, wisdom, choice, and responsibility.

There is no way to detach from responsibility; it is inherent in the universal system. One can avoid it, deny it, pretend to accept it, even half-accept it, but once you understand what a conscious entity's responsibility is, it is best to accept it and abide by it for the sake of all consciousness. If the people on Earth stopped for one moment, took a breath, and thought, "I need to be at peace, full of love, and spread joy," it would be possible to raise the entire human race and all species to the next frequency, and ascend.

The Universe is an exceptionally large place, not just physically, but mentally. Physicists talk about multiple dimensions, multiple worlds, multiple versions of yourself in different worlds in multiple dimensions. Thinking about it is like Alice going down the rabbit hole, it just does not end. The well is very deep, infinite... conscious existence can be thought of as infinite. I see the complexities of dimensions and worlds when I meditate on the Universe. From lifetime to lifetime, our consciousness changes energy form. Each life is another adventure, another learning experience about our environment/dimension and oneself.

The Beginning

When I became self-aware as a child, I knew the universal truths *and* I knew that earthly civilization was not functioning in those truths. I began asking for guidance on how to understand life on Earth, but there was no answer from the Universe and no human seemed to give an acceptable answer; their answers had no spirit, no light in them, just materialism and avoidance.

I was strong-willed with a purpose, and so began my journey to understand how the world functioned. I read many books; it was the late sixties and the hippie movement was in full swing. While there was acceptance in this movement, the United States' systems still did not acknowledge these "new thoughts" as valid. One had to go to the college campus, or leave the country and travel to India, to be in a culture of acceptance, awareness, and meditation. I was too young to leave the country and had to get along the best I could.

The Universe did not completely stay silent with me. At night, lying in bed, I would feel a squeezing pressure around my body and hear a high-pitched sound. It felt comforting. I felt so lost I would beg for the Universe to tell me how to act and what to do. My family was of no assistance; just anger and fighting. Friends were not really friends, just competition. School gave me focus and purpose, and I did well, but it still was not the answer I was seeking. My mind never stopped thinking, trying to figure out existence. I knew this world was not functioning the right way—I knew it was not the way "we" believed. I innately knew I had just come from another life and the ethics and morals were different there than from what I was experiencing on Earth... *Why? What am I supposed to do? How am I supposed to do it? When and where will I find out?*

My bed was where I was closest to the Universe; all my communication took place there, reading books during waking hours, and dreaming during sleeping hours. I was great at daydreaming, going on all kinds of adventures with all kinds of people. At night, I had dreams that were as real as my waking state. In the mornings, I was always tired and did not want to get out of bed. In these dreams I would sleep and have dreams, wake up in the dream, and remember them. I also experienced continuous storylines running in my dream's dream and also remembered them. I think that I lived multiple lives all at once. It is a strange concept to be dreaming and awaken in that dream, then suddenly realize, "I remember this part from a prior dream a few months ago," then have all the memories instantly flood back into consciousness and know you are asleep, dreaming about a dream. It was information overload.

In sixth grade, we had a reading challenge: to read as many books as possible in a month. First, I read Uell Stanley Andersen's *Three Magic Words,* then Aldous Huxley's *Brave New World,* and then

Alive by Piers Paul Read, which is about the Uruguayan rugby union team's survival in the Andes plane crash in 1972. I had no idea what these books were about; I just chose them intuitively. The Universe was talking to me, using a different way of communication. *Three Magic Words* is about one holistic existence. *Brave New World* describes mind/behavior control and rejecting it for freedom. *Alive* was about raw survival. I understood all these stories and saw the truth in them.

Then I began to develop the ability of knowing who was calling on the phone, (this was prior to cell phones and caller IDs). I can also think about someone, and they will call me within a few minutes. Scientifically, this is quantum entanglement. One day soon, everyone will understand that science and spirituality are not opposites but one and the same, and of the whole. I am connected to all, but I have a stronger connection to those sparks and Beings with which I constantly reincarnate. I also know when close friends have passed from this life. They visit me while I am dreaming or sometimes, while I am awake, an event occurs which is specifically related to that person and I just *know*. I have also had people I do not know, or even think about, pass—and when I hear the news, it hits my heart hard, memories of a past life with that person come rushing in, and I feel like I have lost my best friend.

Not Just Mental Masturbation

Knowing how things function is incredibly important to me. There is a stable foundation to existence at any level. While most speak of light, love, and peace—which is desirable and great—I need to understand how light, love, and peace function. Transformation and transcendence: I understand they are real, but I want to know *how* they function, and what the process is. I have the need to understand and share so all entities can come along together.

In college, I majored in Philosophy and took as many esoteric, religious, and logic classes as I could. I also spent time together with the physicists because I knew there were answers for my philosophical questions there. I always thought Philosophy should be practical and "model-able" not just abstract thoughts or "mental masturbation" as it was referred to in school. To demonstrate this, I led the metaphysics class in a meditation of an abstract thought and made a 3D model of Karma and Reincarnation. Philosophy was not just mental masturbation for me. I am now recreating my 3D model of Karma and Reincarnation in a Virtual Reality application/game titled *Rec Room* and have set up a Roman colosseum room with the ability to show presentations and give workshops.

I love technology and have always been a "futurist." I can be in the future, see all the tech, and know I have lived in this futuristic city before. As a result, I know what tech is important for the future of humankind. I remember when I knew time travel had just become possible—and when I knew the transporter from Star Trek had come into existence. When something like this happens, I feel a shift in energy… it's the vibration of the timeline changing when a significant event occurs.

In school, we learned the five "W's": Why, What, Where, When, and How… Wait, one of these is not like the other. My perfect order is not so perfect, but I guess as long as it has a "w" somewhere, it still counts. This still bothers me to this day, but these five words are more important than a perfect category. These five concepts are the path to understanding, freedom, and wisdom. If people used these words for every decision and with integrity and authenticity, there would not be as much negativity, or as many inhumane systems. Once you know, it is hard to go back and pretend you do not. Taking actions with knowledge of harm to people and the planet is irresponsible—and karma does exist.

Our earthly systems have been set up dualistically; inherently, they promote winners and losers, us versus them, good and bad, rich or poor, science versus spirituality, and war or peace. This system of duality also inherently denies anything outside the dualism e.g., liberalism, or gender, or sexuality, or shades of gray. "You are just wasting your vote, taking it away from one of the real parties, Republican or Democrat," as I have been told by so many people when I vote for the third-party candidate.

By implementing a "black and white" perspective that worked incredibly well in task management—I did the task or not, I completed it on time or not, and so on—I discovered I was very task oriented. I accomplished so much and used my meditations with the Universe to pick projects no one was working on so I could be on the bleeding edge of technology. Ideas came to me about new infrastructure architectures with certain technologies, and I would write up the documents on processes, configurations, and classes to train my co-workers. I traveled around the world, collaborating with people at all levels of life and in diverse cultures and industries.

But my "black and white" view of life began to add a little more gray into the mix when I began to work on the business side, not just technology. Business was more about the people and relationships—this was a challenge for me. While I understood the gray nature, I felt inauthentic because the root of the business was "profit or no profit," it was not about real relationships with people. It was about "How I can get you to do what I want you to do so I can get more money." Public organizations were no different; the individuals were after power. All of these systems and people were stuck in this merry-go-round of spirit-killing games. It is not the only way; there are other ways.

A Jazz Song

When I meet someone of significance to me, during the first meeting I see a past life we shared together. Some lives have been on planet Earth, while others involved different constellations and different species. I have been all genders, races, religions, and philosophical systems. The system of existence is not dualistic, but holistic with freedom of choice. How would we learn anything if we did not have freedom of choice?

I know my next life as a conscious entity will be to manage the physics of a solar system. Think about how a solar system functions, with everything spinning exactly the way it needs to keep the system in balance. Life begins to develop on a few planets: you must all keep spinning exactly right, balanced so life can flourish. It is a privilege to be the caretaker for this system. It will last millions of years, but time moves differently in different states of being.

I think of the Universe as a jazz song—it has consistency overall, but throws some wildly different chaotic thoughts into the mix. It's unpredictable, with a little of this instrument, a little of that, and now, all together. It is inclusive, diverse, in your face, and can be fast or slow to rise. It can be almost silent, and then loud and crashing. It is an emotional rollercoaster that can take the known and ordinary and transform it into a new experience. Jazz speaks to my spark of light.

Speaking as Firestarr:

There are many experiences for individual, conscious entities to experience. The spark that is you, never dies; it goes back to the source after each life to do a memory dump, rest, and be cleared for your next experience. We are in a Consciousness System. You are a spark of the Source and are separated from Source to go out into one of the many dimensions, worlds, or space systems to experience and bring back data, information, wisdom, emotions, and experiences to contribute to Source. While away from Source, you are still connected, but you need to be able to experience without influence from Source so your experience can be new and authentic. This is why we do not always remember our past lives and seem to be disconnected from Source. Not everything is perfect, good, and just—or how would we learn?

If you are looking for an answer to the why or how of the Source, the Prime Mover–the First Cause of Everything, there is no answer. We are too far removed from the beginning to know or obtain any information about the First Cause. Consciousness is infinite and time is an illusion, but never ends. Just know that you are infinite, you are conscious, and you are a part of a greater whole. Remember that the whole is more than the sum of its parts.

Right now, there is an opportunity to reconnect. Transcendence is taking place on planet Earth and in the chaos comes transformation— of a new way of thinking, speaking, acting, and being. We do create our own reality. Together on Earth, we—the people—will create a new future world which will partake in the Galactic Federation. Yes, there are other species on other planets, and from other dimensions. It might seem crazy to think about movies and TV shows like Star Trek, Star Wars, Fringe, The Expanse, Avatar, Aliens, Predator, The Magicians, Buck Rogers, Battlestar Galactica, The X Files, *and* Marvel *and* DC *shows as being based on a reality, but it is all possible. Consciousness is potential—everything can exist and not exist at the same time.*

The Conclusion

We are light consciousness and travel from life to life. In this third dimension of the material, we deal with physical bodies, physical things, and we are here to understand the physical.

If you are partially awakened and remember that you are an energy being, a light being, you may find yourself wanting to soar out into the Universe into other dimensions to meet other beings. Your physical body is stuck in 3D space, and it can be a struggle between the two forces—one physical and one light—but you must learn how to integrate the two *and* separate the two. They are both aspects of your current conscious existence. This is a learning Universe, it is teaching you all about itself and yourself; once you learn the lessons, you will be able to travel physically and mentally, and meet other conscious entities. In the vein of Shakespeare's, "All the world's a stage, and all the men and women merely players," (As You Like It, Act 2, Scene 7), the Universe is the entire stage for all of us to play on.

What is interesting is our earthly/human-centric language. I want to say, "We must create a humanity-centric system, not an economic-centric system." "Humanity"—how does that word apply to every conscious entity in the Universe(s)? As long as we only hear, speak, and write, rather than use telepathy, we need new words and concepts to describe outside the human experience. Telepaths do not use words, only emotions and images. Their communication is exact, there is no interpreting what they mean, or what something looks like, because you see it. Until we can become telepathic, we should review our language for descriptions of earthly and universal matters... and open our perspective to be inclusive of what we do not know. In this exercise, we prove that we can see beyond our own thoughts and world. We begin to transform and prepare for the potential of other world species and contact. When our words are exact, our thoughts will follow, and our telepathic images will be consistent, so we can be authentic with our telepathy.

Preparation, practice, and learning are all necessary to work towards transcendence. There is a process, many processes. While chaos has some patterns to it, it still is chaos. Chaos has its purpose and to know when, where, why, what, and how is the wisdom. Chaos is a force used for change/transformation. The Universe does have laws and processes so existence can exist and experience. There are practices I do to prepare myself.

How I Keep On My Path

Meditation of the Chakra System is a fantastic way to begin to connect with your core being. The being that is not physical, that exists in different dimensions. It is a way to start to understand our true selves and connect with the universal consciousness that Carl Jung and Rubert Sheldrake have written about.

Another practice to connect is Qi Gong; since everything that exists is energy, learning to feel the energy around you, and move it, is a good exercise. We are an energy being, our material body is made of energy, so performing Qi Gong to help move the energy, internally and externally, and can help the energy become free-flowing and undo blocks. Once we are free-flowing, we can become one with Universal energy.

In Third-dimensional reality on Earth, we perceive ourselves to be separated from each other, from the earth, from the energy, and from the Universe. The goal is to become one again. Understanding oneness of the Universe, understanding you are everything and nothing (no-thing) at the same time, will lead you on a path of understanding.

Mantra

I am one-ness. I am everything and no-thing. I have no dualism. I am consciousness, I am light, I am energy, I exist. I am.

Dualism exists in Third-dimensional space as one of the constructs that keeps the structure, foundation, coherence, or conformity for this dimension. It is a stepping stone to understand that you cannot have all black and understand it without also having white. It takes the other to understand the one, and understanding that they both exist within the whole. Once you get past the whole, you step into the next dimension, the next frequency.

We humans living in the Third-dimensional world become distracted in its systems and think we do not have time for ourselves, our path, and our metaphysical endeavors. What is life if not my conscious energy, passions, and pursuit of answers to the most important question: What is the meaning of my existence? It is not selfish to focus on oneself. By focusing on oneself, understanding oneself, making choices, thinking about thoughts, words, and deeds, we develop into the type of being we choose to be. Imagine that every other conscious entity is following the same path; there is no time for interfering in others' lives, or fighting, rather, there is time for inner-reflection and gaining understanding, knowledge, and wisdom about ourselves and the world around us. When every entity understands itself, this consistency of thought, word, and deed, think about how that manifests in the Third dimension; does it manifest into chaos, order, peace, cooperation, understanding? Does the Third-dimension transcend into the fourth, fifth, or sixth dimension? We are potential; anything is possible.

Through meditation, we can expand our consciousness; with Qi Gong, we can move energy. When the two practices combine, we are a conscious moving energy force in all dimensions. Where can you go, how much can you learn, see, and improve, and who or what you can be. (There are those 5 W's again.)

Here is the one message I have received from the Universe for my entire life on Earth:

Every conscious being right now, STOP everything, just sit, and take a deep breath, breathe in a count of four, hold a count of four, release your breath a count of four, and hold a count of four. Do this exercise two more times.

You are stillness, you are calm, you are at peace. You have the choice of how you think, speak, and act in this moment. You are doing it now, in the moment—being calm, at peace. You need no thoughts, no speech, no action just being in this state now. All beings, just being now, moment after moment. Reset yourself to—just being now.

Next, begin to think how you want to be in your life, home, neighborhood, city, state, country, world, and Universe. Every morning, begin your day from the breaths, to being, to how you want to be in the next moments of the day in all aspects.

Every conscious being—just being—vibrating with peace and calmness...

ABOUT THE AUTHOR

Yolanda K Dickinson is a Capricorn who climbs every mountain asking, "Where's the next one?" well before she has reached the summit. Her busy life is filled with learning as much as she can about existence. Born a philosopher with a priori knowledge, Yolanda is a jack-of-all-trades trying to be a master of life.

A native of Colorado, she has been fortunate to travel nationally and internationally for her work in IT with IBM. She holds a Bachelor of Arts in Philosophy with a minor in Psychology, a Master of Science in Management of Information Systems, a Master of Science in Acupuncture, a Doctorate of Ministry, and authored a patent in IT cloud framework.

Yolanda's passion is philosophy, specifically esoteric metaphysics. Philosophy was her path to questioning the Universe, Earth, and human civilization. Her core belief is that "People should never stop thinking and asking questions about life and our reality." When she was young, the universe began communicating with her; she calls that voice Firestarr.

At home, she cares for dogs of all breeds, works in the yard, and plays and builds new environments in Virtual Reality.

Founder of *Bamboo n Lotus Wellness Consulting*, Yolanda is a Wellness Coach who provides services in: Akashic Records, Guided Meditations, Vibrational Sound services, Energy work, Chaldean Numerology, Blended Essential Oils, and workshops on a variety of topics. Her current running workshop is *The Source Training*; a journey through your life, the world, and the Universe to promote optimal mental and physical wellness.

- Email: yolanda@bamboonlotus.clinic
- Website: https://bamboonlotus.clinic
- Facebook: Bamboo Lotus

The Path Reveals Itself

"ILLUMINATING THE PATH" WITH WORDS OF WISDOM

CHANNELED BY VIRGINIA SADA YORK

*W*ords.

The power of them.

The delight and poetry of them.

The impact of them.

How we reach each other as humans.

Words are central to our existence.

Some are thought about, shaped, treasured, intentional.

Others are flung about, with insensitivity or taken for granted.

Still others flow, seem natural, have potency and magnetise us;

Speak to the heart of things;

Are crystal clear, imbued with wisdom and sharp clarity.

"ILLUMINATING THE PATH" WITH WORDS OF WISDOM

I had to travel deep into life before learning my words did affect people. While I am still learning this, and am often not mindful enough when I use words, slowly I began to see something had started to happen in my work as coach and therapist.

My executive coaching style uses "conversational learning" to develop insight with the coachees. Increasingly, I found people "hanging off" every word I said, repeating back what I had said months or years before, letting me know that words I had spoken had touched or changed them.

I always check whether reflections or words I share have resonance, and the resounding, "Yes! That is uncanny, how do you know?" became louder and louder!

This made me think deeply about the impact of words shared. And while I have always used quotes purposefully and instructionally from other people—"Be the change you desire." (Gandhi) and "Let your work be your art." (Rumi)—my own sayings became quotes as I became sure of these axioms and started to quote myself!

Awakening to increasingly using my intuition, I learned to let wisdom flow from "beyond logic." I find that people are often too busy to read as they have become so used to receiving an overwhelming amount of input from scanning and scrolling, and now are often unable to concentrate for long periods. Over time, it became clear that part of my function is to read, summarise, condense research into blasts of wisdom, and share these as potent messages for clients from the Universe!

I never thought of myself as a "channel." I never thought of myself as an Oracle.

This all felt in the realm of people much more "inter-dimensional" or psychic than me! I have had some contact with the "other side," particularly with family members who have passed over, but "channelling" was something angelic ethereal people do—not me!

My practice of being in an aligned and centred state before each session has become much more intentional over the years. I increased my focus on being open and ready before each session by using sprays, meditation, readings, mantras, and breathing practices, plus setting intentions to get myself into a calm, open, and available space before each session. Increasingly, I feel I speak to clients from intuition, from a flow stage of perception, that is more profoundly focused on being of service to the process of the other person.

As the years have gone by, I have developed deep confidence that the words and insights I offer are highly attuned to each person I work with. I am in contact with conscious opening to my Higher Self, to allow words that are totally unrehearsed to pour through me. I began to trust that my voice is needed.

And meanwhile, in my own life, I have more contact with beloved ones who have passed over. I have a more vibrant relationship with the Divine on a daily basis. I feel connected to the Goddess, within and without. I trust the unseen spirit realm. And then, there is Delphi.

Experience at Delphi

The first time I went to Delphi I was very young, a student of history. The most recent—and third—visit was on the honeymoon of my second marriage, and I delighted in being back in a place that feels so familiar to me.

It was on my second visit to Delphi, by myself in 2012, that I had a huge awakening including flashbacks to ancient days. Transfixed and intrigued, I wanted to find where the Oracle worked from, and was in a trance of ancient energy, in an otherworldly dream state, as I sat for hours in the quiet at the Temple of Apollo.

Surprisingly, it became clear I had been a Delphi Oracle! There were many, not just one, and much has been written about the trance state induced by the underground vapours of Mount Parnassus that affected each Oracle. Interestingly, these days I note that Delphi Priests "interpreted" for the Priestess.

Unlike the Oracle Priestesses, I do not need men to interpret my messages. I will make them clear to you myself! With my deep respect for the development of philosophy, education, therapy, theatre, and more from the Ancient Greek world, I am utterly drawn to all things Greek. This past life link makes sense of my respect, love, and complete feeling of being at home in Greece. "Ancient Ways for Modern Days" is one of my taglines—it honours the deep wisdom that carries forth from all forms of ancient wisdom-based practices.

An Oracle Path

As time has passed in my coaching and counselling work, I have found myself "overtaken" often, with words coming with ease as I work with clients—and without much analysis. When I check in with them, my clients often say of what I have spoken, "That is so spot on, that speaks to me *so* clearly."

Intuitive writing and speaking have become my everyday experience. Yes, I am trained in many modalities and can refer to scholarly and evidential works with ease. However, a deeper or higher *knowing* pours through me often.

I know it's not me. It is higher intelligence that arrives succinctly, wanting to be heard. I feel possessed, though not in a frenzy! I describe it as being in the grip of a force of insight - speaking, challenging, and bringing words in easy flow to assist others.

An Oracle has messages, words.

An Oracle has insight.

I don't force, I flow.

I don't judge, I offer.

I don't decide, I extend.

It is all an offering.

An Oracle gives messages for those who ask.

An Oracle gives wise or authoritative opinions.

An Oracle gives insight, wise counsel, even prophetic predictions. Socrates said the Delphic Oracle was "an essential guide to personal and state development."

So there have always been Oracles, sought out for advice. Maybe this shows the eternal human need for inspired advice from other realms.

I accept now that I can offer words that do help people; my pattern-seeing, future-sensing, light-holding gives hope and pathways to those I speak with.

I accept that words I speak or write have resonance and influence.

I lean into intuition now, to being "led" to say things.

I revere the supreme universal intelligence we share through our art, words, and relationships.

So, I trust the experience of words as power.

I trust the intentional use of messaging, the impact of language, the energy of the word.

Yes, I will Oracle for you.

My Learnings

1. Trust

As I became more experienced, I began to trust the process of allowing intuitive flow. I began to own the wisdom earned from my own immense challenge and, at times, suffering. I delighted that I could illuminate a path for clients, that I could happily share wisdom and offer insights that were on the mark… so clients could see and know what they needed to move forward.

But it took a while to consciously *know* I was opening to another dimension, and realise that the words were flowing so strongly at times that this was not insight I had ownership of—not what I was thinking about in my logical mind but more akin to intuition or channelling.

So I have begun to explore this more, relaxing into the way I open and prepare for each session (though of course, I do read my session notes and attune to the person as part of my personal preparation). I have my own tools for opening the channel, for being centred, and for accessing my psychic powers. I consciously connect to Source, or divine intelligence. And the Goddess.

Our culture, now, doesn't directly talk about, nor value, what "inspiration" is!

In-spired is a state. Of an invisible energy or spirit filling us or leading our energy. I feel inspired to let the words from a higher self or higher place pass through me. It is humbling. It is not ego-led.

I began to know I was bridging two worlds, increasingly talking about the visible and invisible worlds, myth, spirituality, and navigating the mysteries with my clients. Many of them live in the pragmatic, structured world of analysis and problem-solving that is big business. But so much isn't working or in "ease" for them, so another language was needed and seems to have resonance.

During much of my daily life, I think about communication, flow and connection, and the rising energy of the feminine on the planet. This offers the world differing insights, rebalancing and healing energy, and expression from the heart-centre rather than ego.

I can intuitively channel messages people need to hear and offer the guidance they often crave at a soul level. It seems unconventional but we all need higher sources of inspiration... and other dimensions of knowing can be so incisive and apt. Insight can be strident, or soft.

Calm or cutting through illusion. Yin and Yang, masculine and feminine energies, are the great dance of difference.

Now, I feel empowered with so much connection to the Oracle of Delphi running through me since my second visit to the site of the Delphic Oracle, below the Temple of Apollo in Delphi. Also, The Sanctuary of Athena blew me away—and into another time zone! Truly magical other-worldly realms came as a flashback to me… and talk about "inner knowing!" Transfixed, while I sat alone at the site for many hours, I didn't want to leave. I felt I was home.

2. Letting My Voice Through

I am not scared of my voice. I am not scared to use it.

I used to be scared to speak my truth when I was younger.

I held myself back, even in my forties! Slowly, I began to trust my insights and now, many years later, I know my voice is needed and heard.

There is no ego with an Oracle. The message is for the receiver.

It is of benefit for the audience, for the one who asked for help.

3. Lineage and Respect

I learn from others of all ages and all races. I stay open to being an active learner.

I respect my teachers and the great lineages of family and teachers who brought me to this point in my life.

I bow down to my teachers, the goddesses and wise ones lighting my path, and for that I am grateful. Though I have learnt that, eventually, we must pioneer our own path (learnt through tests and failings as much as successes), it is important and healthy to recognise those who have, and do, inspire us!

My inspiring goddesses are Athena, Aphrodite, Hera, and Persephone. Quan Yin and Tara.

These female deities are held and honoured as aspects of myself. And lately, Mary Magdalene is calling, and so does Delphi from long ago times.

Teachers, inspirers, and mentors include Dr Marcia Leventhal, Min Mia, Jean Houston, Joanna Macey, Isadora Duncan, Virginia Woolf, Charmian Clift, Anais Nin, Dianne Stein—all writers, activists, teachers, and pioneers in their fields.

My Message For You:

Let what wants to come through speak to you, resonate with you.

Whatever is meant for you will touch you.

I GIVE YOU THESE WORDS now, for YOUR benefit.

1. What Can I Forsee?

While there have always been times of challenge for humans in our history on Earth, now is an especially insidious time—of disempowerment, loss of culture, confused thinking, unhealthy practices with the body, and centralising control forces. There is struggle and collapse as strain increases and institutions dissolve.

Dehumanising and greedy forces are strong. Loss of personal agency may threaten. Loss of ability to focus or have strong memory and clarity is increasing. Making wise choices for health and self-agency may seem diminished in the deluge of over-informed distraction. There is increasing chaos and collapse.

But rather than hovering too long in these dark energies, reclaim your own centre, keep your inner light clear, and focus upon healing, transforming, and being potent human beings. Spend time now to dream and imagine, and allow change to come. Be brave in the Void, and let what emerges lead you.

Stay connected and anchored in your divine nature.

Heaven and Earth meet in the human form. We are indeed spiritual beings having earthly experiences and we hold the creative power to make our reality!

Move towards each other and develop communities of support.

Move inside and develop your inner resources.

Move outwardly to create the new.

2. What You Need To Do

Trust Yourself

You might as well be yourself—everyone else is taken!

Famous words.

Knowing how to be potent, effective, and heard is still so affected by the patriarchal inheritances on this planet.

Think of the sort of woman you want to be. It may be hard to find role models or teachers, but seek them out.

You will find more pleasure, ease, and flow being the woman you truly are.

So experiment.

Be brave.

Be authentic.

I want to encourage you to use the time on this planet to live fully, to live creatively, to live out loud. In an idiosyncratic, original, imaginative way. Love your differences. Trust your ability to create—at home, in relationships, in your art, in your business. Manifest and create—this is your divine yet human power.

Let Your Body Be Your Spiritual Practice

You have a human form and need to remember this. It is not a problem—it is a blessing, so use your body like it IS a temple.

What you put in it, what you access—it's all experienced through the body.

So good water is vital, and good food, as organic as possible.

Don't overload the body, with food or experiences, with chemicals or exhaustion!

Let it be nourished but also free to move.

Make sure you get clear which practices support your well-being.

Daily habits may not all be healthy ones. A habit can rule you.

Practices are more conscious choices. Intention and discipline are part of practices—like practising how to play the piano or how to swing a golf club. Practice is vital to aligned achievement, to success and fulfilment. To living a conscious life. Think: What are the practices that bring you joy and meaning?

Becoming more intentional and keeping your body, vessel, psyche, heart and mind clear in these enormous days of change on planet Earth is vital to the awakening and uplevelling that is happening in the consciousness of the planet.

Watch your thoughts and words spoken with vigilance. You create energy with your words, so be sure of what you want to create. It will change what you speak out into space.

Move Your Body

Too much sitting and lack of sunlight just isn't good for your blessed vehicle. You need to remember that these times you live in are very stimulating to the mind, but the body is left behind! Too much head energy gets confusing and overly analytic.

Make space to be still and quiet, and rest. Be with others when you need that. But be in solitude more, so you can feed your soul and pay attention to your life.

There is a schema of distraction in the modern, developed, consumer world of overloads of information and misinformation.

Return to natural materials and practices that honour all life on Earth and basic principles of existence, such as love, compassion, learning, attraction, and being with tribe.

And then make space to be expressive, not just taking in "information," but expressing outwardly—creatively sharing your responses, your imagination, your inner truths.

And don't forget: Dance is a wonderful way to release energy held in the body. The non-verbal path of dance allows release, recharging, rejuvenation, and seeing what your body is trying to tell you!

Honour The Interdependence Of All Things

We humans are born but cannot thrive without the holding and assistance of parents and others. Unlike a baby horse or elephant, which is up and exploring movement and moving with the herd within hours or days of being born, the human infant is totally dependent.

We are interdependent beings; we depend on the sun for photosynthesis, on each other to help make our dwellings, on bees for pollination of our crops, on people who make roads, or food, or clothing ... We are never IN-dependent of others.

We are woven into the fabric of life together—with microbes, whales, butterflies—and are finding now that we can measure interdependence. The fine but strong web of connection.

So, humbly knowing we need each other to get through difficult times with each other, the interdependent nature of human life becomes revered.

Trust Your Intelligence

Humans have amazing levels of intelligence to tap into.

Follow and trust your *human* intelligence, not *artificial* intelligence (AI). You have all you need, and you can access so much more through higher knowing.

Humans also have multiple intelligences—with social, emotional, spiritual, and many more intelligences on tap. Humans don't need deluges of the data of the past to make decisions for the future. You have your imagination! You still barely use all the possibilities of your intelligences.

AI collects the past known, or projects from supposition, but human intelligence can create, be inspired from the unknown, and work with mystery, intuition, magic, and play to endlessly create.

Use Your Imagination—It Encircles The Universe

Our creative abilities are superb and vital to humans—so keep using them!

Imagine

Imagine a world where living is not divided into business and pleasure. Work and freedom.

Where what you create or make is valued and you barter/exchange/get money for doing it.

Where work is beauty, and hence, full of joy and flow and what you love to do.

Imagine

Imagine a world where the good of all—humans, animals, earth, water, air, all levels of life—is considered in every product made or every venture. Choices are made based upon, "Is this healthy for all humans? Is this healthy for the environment?"

Imagine

Imagine a Council of Elders who discuss and decide. Like Jedi warriors, they are highly trained, with no reward other than service. It is their spiritual duty to set criteria and bless ventures. To teach principles of leading and service.

Imagine

Imagine leading change and creativity in your suburb, family, or workplace, focused upon conscious compassion and caring decisions.

Imagine

Imagine never forgetting you are loved.

Imagine never forgetting you can create.

Imagine never forgetting you are Source/God/Universal Intelligence in human form.

"I am enough of an artist to draw freely upon my imagination. Imagination is more important than knowledge. Knowledge is limited. Imagination encircles the world."

Albert Einstein

Be In Solitude

"In ancient times... solitude was used as an oracle, as a way of listening to the inner self to solicit advice and guidance otherwise impossible to hear in the din of daily life."

"ILLUMINATING THE PATH" WITH WORDS OF WISDOM

Clarissa Pinkola Estes

Our neon world is over-stimulating and overwhelming.

Withdraw. Often.

Turn off the devices and the continual interference with your own inner process.

Be best friends with your spirit! Spend time in enquiry in your interior world.

In the quiet we can sense our place, our feelings, our connections, our questions.

We need quiet times daily for insight to arrive, to unpack feelings and reactions, to dwell in calm energy and let our nervous systems replenish and renew.

Be Priestess Of Yourself

Self-affirming, self-sovereign, be in trust of yourself. Giving decisions away to someone else is losing your power. Command what you desire, be what you desire, purify yourself for your own benefit, and for increasing the impact of your work and wisdom in the world.

Use your powers of intentionality and manifestation. There is much to heal, starting with ourselves. At this time it is palpable that Gaia, Goddess, Creatrix energies are activated. The energy of the rising feminine is helping women be empowered, uniquely feminine, focused on healing, expression, connection and healthy community. The capacity to align the crown, third eye, heart, solar plexus, and root chakra, and keep feet on the ground, is immense in the inner priestess of every woman.

Embrace your two aspects—human and divine, light and dark,

shadow and seen, solar and lunar. Be aware of this and unify your energy.

Choose Light.

Choose what Love would do next.

Use Your Voice

I speak this especially to women, at this time on planet Earth, as the Divine Feminine is rising. The Patriarchy has been a ruling system and belief set on Earth, but its days are waning. We step away from empowering the Patriarchy by not participating in it!

Everywhere I find women acknowledging their experience of the Feminine Rising. It really is time to own your own path! We have enormous capacity to use imagination and dreams to fuel our desires —to skilfully and potently create newness.

New conscious business realms, new ways of organisation, new community connections, new ways of relationship—the awakening to a new level of existence will mean leaving the existing Matrix behind and living from deep and high consciousness. Intentionality, heart and mind alignment, clarity, creativity, and imagination will be used increasingly to create ground-breaking and mind-blowing days ahead.

And especially Women, your voices are needed!

To calm, to share insight, to sing, to speak out, to affect change, to extend potency in the world. You will learn the art of expansion—not reducing, not living in fear, not playing small.

Live with your full Eros, your full heart wisdom, expressing into the world.

The Voice of the Feminine is loud now, and potent.

I was "overtaken" in a kind of trance state as I wrote this poem:

THE VOICE OF THE GODDESS

By Virginia Sada York

July, 2023

The Voice of the Goddess

Is no paltry whisper.

She is screaming now.

Medusa.

Banshee.

Hysteria.

The Furies.

This pure ice.

This burning flame.

This "No!"

This Roar.

This sword now raised

In blinding potent light.

Not to kill Male,

But to cut through illusion.

To dismember oppression, greed and arrogance.

To empower women.

To redress wrongs.

To break the capitalist, patriarchal containment lines.

To free the women of wellbeing, of healing herbs,

And wise midwifery

From the stake.

To kill the Darkness.

You may be deaf

But you WILL feel the rumble

In archaeological plates of earth,

Tectonically shifting,

In a roar of release,

A smash of disarray,

A bursting explosion of the baby

From the womb of the world.

The galaxy's holding

No longer able

To contain

The power of the Goddess.

This dangerous diamond of clarity and cutting.

This vocal strength of screaming pain.

This overwhelming

Uncontainable

Might and pureness,

In the roar of Her Voice,

Birthing herself anew.

So Please, Question Yourself:

1. What if change wasn't "bad," or "fear-inducing?"

2. What if it all worked out? Knowing this, how would I show up?

3. What gifts/talents/assets do I have to offer to the world?

4. What if I fully trusted myself and my intuitive knowing?

These times are profound as the collective is healing and elevating into a new consciousness. The time is rich to create our new world—with all limitations and unhealthy beliefs, patterns, habits, and mental and institutional limits dispelled.

Intensify your practices.

Lean into your inter-woven, interdependent relationships.

Be *in* the world, but not *of* it.

Live between the two worlds, visible and invisible.

Lead your life with Grace and Beauty, and remember and use your ability and choice to create.

These words are intended to clarify and inspire.

To remind you of principles and practices to help you with the wisdom choices you make to create your Path.

It is all unfolding and emerging.

ABOUT THE AUTHOR

Virginia Sada York is a transformative coach and therapist, catalysing learning and change in organisations and individuals. Her unique methods combine her passion for metaphysics, energetics, mindfulness, and creativity in her potent roles of teacher, coach, writer, dancer, and poet.

Trained in literature, education and media, somatic psychotherapy, martial arts, and dance movement therapy, she is highly experienced in activating transformation, leadership learning, and conscious awakening.

For over twenty years her global coaching practice, Your World Within, has helped leaders from all sectors to expand their potential. Using mindfulness, positive psychology, and healing modalities, Virginia speaks to artfully navigate major changes in life or career, helping clients find purpose and passion.

Her newest program, The Poiesis Path, pioneers an uplifting combination of ancient wisdom, creativity practice, and tangible strategy for female artists, healers, leaders, and small business entrepreneurs to confidently create their desired world.

- Email: virginiasadayork@gmail.com
- Website: www.virginiasadayork.com
- LinkedIn: Virginia Sada York
- Facebook: https:www.facebook.com/virginia.s.york

We Evolve

REVOLUTION EVOLUTION

CHANNELED BY LEN BLEA

It started around eight-years-old. I was standing there, by myself, and everything around me turned white. I didn't know where I was or what was happening. Then I looked up and saw Jesus on the cross; I was witnessing the crucifixion. As I witnessed it, Jesus and I were the only two in existence. After that moment, everything around me reappeared as it was. Later on, I saw visions of chariots, fighting, war, and other scenarios. These snippets happened whenever and wherever and, at the time, I didn't know that these were visions of past lives.

Around this time, I was also scrying, although I didn't know it was called "scrying" until ten years ago. Scrying is a practice of focusing on a mirror or other object to receive visions of the future. During one of my scrying episodes, I told my sister that there was a green van that caused an accident, and it was horrible. I said to Tina, "Why can't you see it?" In response, she grabbed me by the shoulders and shook me, saying, "Len, that's not happening." As soon as she said this, I saw myself as an adult in a straight jacket in an institution. From this moment on, I never again talked about what I saw in the mirror.

A few months later I saw my first ghost; I was as frightened as can be because he would stand next to the bed at night and taunt me. I was also able to do hands-on healing, but I didn't know what it was called. When I touched someone's head, I could take their headache away, although I would unintentionally absorb it. The next day, I always had a headache, then it would disappear.

These experiences continued throughout my teenage years and into my twenties. I didn't know that all these gifts were from the Universe, Spirit, God, and the Divine. When I finally found out, in my early thirties, that they were gifts, I was able to learn how to control them and utilize them in ways that blessed people and stopped the lower vibrations from trying to harm me. Several times, I tried to walk away. But the more I tried to resist these gifts, the more people came in need of my help. Even now, strangers come up to me in stores, restaurants, and public places and share their life stories or issues with me. I tell them what they need to know. The interaction takes place as needed and I never see them again.

I don't believe in coincidence but, rather, in synchronicities and signs. The more I embrace who I am—these gifts and this journey—the more people come. More help is done and I'm in a different mindset. When you *know* that your journey is just to show up and be there for those who need it—that you are simply the middleman/channel—and you say exactly what people need to hear, it's uplifting. It makes me laugh sometimes, because I'm still afraid of the dark and sleep with the lights on because I don't want certain spirits to bother me.

I have been channeling for about ten years now. My connection with the Divine is automatic. After many conversations, I don't remember what I have said; in these past ten years, I have done thousands of combined aura photos, channeled, psychic, medium and energy readings. I have found that everything comes to us in Divine order and timing, which brings about a feeling of empowerment. I believe that we can all channel. All we have to do is get out of our ego, go into our hearts, and remember where we came from. There really is no disconnect between the Divine and ourselves. We are part of the Divine as much as the Divine is a part of us. When we embrace that, the channel becomes so automatic that there is no disconnect. It's as though you're in your body, you're aware of what's going on with your body, you're speaking words that just flow through you; you're exactly where you need to be and the recipient needs to hear everything that is said in those exact words that are spoken. After the channeled reading, not much of the information is remembered as the Divine uses your voice, your body, and your expressions as the messenger. It's a unique and beautiful experience.

The following channeled messages will be received differently by each individual reading them, and they will be received differently each time you read them. Please listen with an open heart, open mind, and love. If you feel floaty, lightheaded, or ungrounded after reading and connecting to them, please remember to ground, drink water, and disconnect from the energy of the channeled reading. Also, please remember to give thanks for the messages and thank Source for providing these messages. Being thankful provides the opportunity for more messages to come through to you, to others, and the collective.

Today I invite all women to take a moment, take a deep breath and close their eyes and just breathe in the Divine. Breathing in the Divine all the way through the body from the crown chakra to the feet. Feeling that connection with Source and really remembering where they came from. Be open to the messages and sensations that come through. As I channel, the message that comes through is this:

Embrace who you are always, for who you are is that of a spirit who seeks an abundance of love, who gives an abundance of love, and who exists with an abundance of love. Can you feel the warmth within your heart, within your hands, flowing through you as though you're a beacon of light? You and the Divine are one. Allow this to circle through you, and feel it. As you feel it, remember you're one with the Divine. Can you see, can you feel, the strength, the warmth, the love, the energy? It swirls and warms you. It connects you. You can access this energy at any time. It's a part of you as much as you are a part of it.

Now I close my eyes and I ask the Divine: What is it that women need to know right now?

I hear the answer:

Embracing who you are, embracing the love, embracing all the humanity regardless of how you're being treated, is what's best right now. Remember your strength, honor your strength, honor yourself, love yourself. There's so much to see.

Although it's temporary, you know why you're here. Step back for a moment and see the picture for what it truly is. Not what you see but the broader spectrum of life and the temporary reality that we live in. When you embrace that it is only temporary, you ease the suffering. When you can embrace the suffering, you can embrace love. You can understand the Yin and Yang, the opposite and the balance that's brought between the two. You can breathe in masculine and feminine energy and you can breathe out strength and love. You can breathe in strength and love and breathe out masculine and feminine energy. For you know and understand that humanity needs you, and this, at this time.

Women are strong, women are fierce, women are an amazing force. This force that you bring will amplify the essence of all of the feminine energy within this world, within the existence within these dimensions. Can you feel it? Surround yourself with this feeling of strength, balance, love, and existence. It's not about competition. It's not about right or wrong. It's about remembering why you are here. It's about embracing the journey and knowing that you chose to be here at this time. It's about remembering where you came from and remembering where you will return to. Let all the false visions, all the false vibrations, all the false realizations, all the false words that you hear, fall from you. As these fall from you, let yourself be filled with positive vibrations, positive realizations, and positive words. May you always remember you're here to empower—as women can bear children, women are the reason we exist. Call in your power of existence, embrace your power of existence, and remember your power of existence.

Thank you for the message.

Next channeled question is: What does humanity need to know right now?

There will always be chaos, negativity, and lower vibration throughout humanity. You have chosen to be here at this time. It's an uplifting time, always. Even through the lower, negative times, there's beauty. Express your emotion, feel it for what it is, and let it go. Look at the lessons that you are given and are receiving, for those are what is important at this time. There's beauty in death, love, joy, honor, sadness, grace, and anxiety. Embrace this beauty. It's like a flower so rooted in the ground that, no matter what happens, it blooms every year. It rebirths every spring with a new bloom of sort. Same plant, same roots, new flowers, new petals, and at the same time, old, recycled energy. It's that old, recycled energy that rejuvenates us to remember the bliss, the love, the joy.

Let go of the expectations of what you thought life was and embrace what it is. An abundance of memories, laughter, tears, screams, rage, love, emotion, hugs, loss, and gains. The balance of it will always remain as long as you remain in balance. You see, it was not really one-sided until you made it that way. You needed it to kilter and off-teeter so you could understand balance. Now if it were smooth sailing, you'd never know the crash of a wave against the boat and that rush of energy feeling that comes with the clash and crash. Can you feel it? It brings up excitement, fear, and hope—and that can be scary, but that's ok because you're in balance.

You'll always be ok. There are lessons behind it all. You've come so far to go even further. Let the expectations fall away and embrace the love that you were given to live this life. Embrace you, your existence, your path, your knowledge, and your weakness. Embrace it all for all exists within you, outside of you and around you. Your reaction to the action is key. So mote it be.

Thank You.

Next question is: What ancient wisdom needs to be shared now?

Take off your mask, expose your true essence. When you expose your true essence, you show who you truly are, not what you think you are. Call in your ancestors for guidance, seek herbs, old traditional ways of healing.

Silence is beautiful. Silence brings beauty. Stop being afraid to know who you are.

Stop making situations with false feelings to not make people angry. Speak your truth. Seek the knowledge from your heart. Speak from your heart. See from your heart. Gaze at it from your heart. Remove society's programming from your mind. Feel. Trust your intuition. Trust your heart. Trust that the Divine trusts in you as much as you should trust in yourself. Let people see you. Let people know you. Your wisdom will come from your heart.

You know your ancestors within this lifetime and those across all dimensions, time, and space. Call upon them to guide you, to uplift you, to remind you that you are not alone. See yourself as one with the Divine. Feel yourself as you are one with the Divine.

Remove all expectations of the outcome and allow it to flow to you, through you, within you, around you, everywhere. If it doesn't feel right, listen. If it doesn't sound right, ignore it. Intuition will never lead you astray. The more you listen and embrace, the more it will race to you. The more it will expand within you. The more you will be able to show others how their intuition helps them.

Remember we are all unique with DNA but we're all the same energetically. One is all, all is one. Seek that deepness within you that you've covered. Open your third eye. Connect to source. Embrace that where you come from and where you are going exist. You're only in this lifetime temporarily for the reasons you may or may not know. Always know you're pure light and love.

Thank You.

The next question is: Would you please provide a channel message that will resonate with present and future readers of this book?

Why do you seek outside of you, when all that is, is always within you? The love is within you, the light is within you. At the end of the day, all there really is, is love. That is your true form. That is where you come from. That is what you will return to.

As light beings and souls, you have forgotten the light within. Spark the light within always. Never forget who you are or where you've come from. Although knowing where you're going is important, it's not always the key or the anchor to your path. You have free will so you can change anything at any time, and that free will always will be your destiny. Chosen people in this chosen time will always succeed no matter what. It's not about ego, it's not about accomplishment, it's about being present. It's about being able to be in the moment all of the time even through the chaos, even through the consistent change, even through the pressure. It's about always being awake even in the dark, even in the constant pressured times. It's about an abundance of love, friendship, growth and spirituality. It's about remembering and embracing this human body. It's not about seeking revenge. It's about keeping the Faith and knowing you're always exactly where you need to be. It's not about broken promises or money or fame. It's not about lust. It's about growth, spirituality, and love. It's about educating and continuing and holding the hands of others as you go forward as a collective, as a consciousness, as a community. It's about putting your best step forward, even when you're not 100%, knowing that everything will be okay. It's about understanding that humanity is and always will exist. It's about embracing change in time and it's about letting go. It's about being okay with letting go. It's okay to be without. It's okay to seek balance. It's okay to fall apart. All will fall apart to fall into place. And on the verge of your crashing and hitting rock bottom, you land on a soft cushion and know that the fall was always worth it.

We don't expect you to always be perfect all of the time because you're perfect with everything you do. We don't see perfection as you do. So if you look at perfection and you look at you, you'll remember you're always perfect. So please continue to seek inside, allow and trust your intuition to guide you. Call on us for help when you seek it. Our signs may be subtle or our signs may be huge, but the signs will be there for you. Always go with peace and love. Never wish harm on others, regardless of how hurt you are—and always, always remember you're loved.

Thank you.

The next question is: Would you please provide any last minute notes, or thoughts, or words that we need to hear at the current moment?

All is within you. All will always be within you. When there is doubt, look within. When there is sadness, look within and remember the lessons and the beauty within everything. As that is who you are—beauty. When it feels like there is a power struggle, go within and remember the Divine has you, Source has you, God has you, Goddess has you.

Gender is fluid, energy is fluid. Time and space are not important. And as it continues to speed up, breathe and go with the flow. Do not be annoyed that you do not have enough time, as everything is in Divine order and timing, always.

Remember who you are. Find your heart and find its center and in doing so you'll remember the love and the light that you are. It is difficult being in the human incarnation form for their feelings, emotions, thoughts, repercussions, and doubts. Although these are here, they do not necessarily define the spirit form that you are. Rather, it helps you to identify that these are temporary feelings, emotions, and states that are needed to be completed to understand your existence as it fully is. Hug yourself, embrace yourself, and thank yourself for being kind enough to yourself, as you have chosen to come down here at this time. During this rough time. It does not define you in the sense of a one-self identity, rather it defines the collective of those who are troubled, those who are loved, those who are in this existence. We are all in this pool of consciousness, and as we remain in this pool of consciousness, we must remember we are here to observe. And to play our roles, and to not become so attached to the outcome, or our emotions will be brought to the surface in a negative way.

The collective energy will always remain in balance with all of the emotions that are within the circular energy. Your heart has never led you astray and your heart will continue to help you to move forward. Take a deep breath in and close your eyes and the red that you see are the emotions, the love, the passion, the anger, the hurts, the joy; all of those emotions are within you. There is love within the anger. There is love within the sadness. There is a place for all of the emotions. There is balance with all of them as well.

We thank you. We smile. We are happy that you were kind, gentle, wise, and strong enough to come down into this human incarnation existence; it's such a time when such strength, humanity, collapsing, chaos, confusion, is clashing. You will move forward ,we will move forward. The only difference between you and us is that shell of the *body. Thank you for going forward, we will be here should you need us. Thank you. Bless you. We love you.*

After a channel, I don't go back to read what was said or to determine if it makes sense because that is not what I need to do. It's not about me, it's about the message that goes through, it's about the message being delivered and received as needed. It's not for me to dissect, correct, or analyze.

We're all here for a reason. Whether we realize it or not isn't significant. There are those who know what their path is, those who question what their path is, and those who don't realize they're already on their path. That's the beauty of living.

Wherever you are, whatever you're doing, whatever has happened, has led you to be the person you are today. Now what you do going forward from your past can imprison you, can free you, can expand you, can uplift you; it can do whatever you want it to do. Your choice will be the right choice. There is no "I should have," no "I could have," or no "I would have." There is only "I did." There is only "I am."

When it feels like it's falling apart, it's falling together—just like a puzzle. The shapes change, the pieces change, the image changes but the puzzle remains. What is an expression and extension of you, is an expression and extension of me. We are the same, yet different. We are unique, yet we are one. Steps are steps, no matter how big, no matter how small. No matter how many forward, or how many back. No matter how long the path. May you find the inner peace you seek. When you find that inner peace, may you share your experience with others, so that they can share theirs and create an amazing, expanded ripple effect of inner peace. It's always in Divine timing and order.

Thank you.

May each and every one of you, and all of us, show up. Speaking the truth is difficult; speak it anyway. Be kind to those who are not necessarily kind to you. Every time someone hurts you, step back as they are showing you their vulnerability. Learn from their vulnerability rather than using it as a weapon against them. Learn from your own vulnerability and use it as a stepping stone so that you can show others vulnerability is strength. Remember who you are and where you came from is where you will return to. It's not easy being human, but it's worth that French silk pie, that kiss from your sibling, the smile of the child that you gave a Band-Aid to when they cut their knee. The small little things that we take for granted are the ones that you really need to be appreciative of, and for. Much love to all of you. May you always blossom, and remember—you are always on the right path. As this part of the chapter closes, I wish all of you well, health, peace, love, and all of the beautiful things that come to you.

I am always thankful for the role I have been given. As long as God, the Universe, Source, the Divine show me how to be and lead me, I will continue the role. I invite you to be open to play your role. It is not about perfection. It is about showing up. Showing up and allowing the connection to take place, giving thanks when it happens, and releasing the process. Gifts are gifts, as roles are roles. Please step into yours. Please step into your role.

Thank you Universe, the Divine, God, Goddess, Source, and all of the light creation, for allowing me to be a channel. Thank you for trusting me to share these words. Thank you for choosing me to share them as they are needed. Thank you for allowing me to be the middleman. Thank you for allowing me to be the messenger.

Thank you. Thank you. Thank you.

ABOUT THE AUTHOR

Len Blea is an energy reader, energy clearer, and holder of space. She channels universal energy and opens and creates a safe space for those during sessions. Having received her gifts at a young age, Len didn't know what to do with them until she became an adult, when she honed in on them and furthered her knowledge. She has worked with men and women to identify the cause of their individual issues, bring it to the surface, and provide suggestions on how to work through it.

When someone is in need, she is there. Len knows that part of her journey is to just show up. She understands that the Universe brings people together as needed, when needed, and for the length of time required for the process to finish. She knows that she cannot, and will not, walk away from her path; this is what she is called to do.

It is difficult to define what occurs during Len's client sessions - and that's ok. All that matters is that Len and her client know that it is an energy flow that happens as it needs to.

- Email: Msmysteriousecho@gmail.com
- Facebook: https://m.facebook.com/LightingLady777/?ref=bookmarks
- Instagram:@lightninglady777

Hear The Voice of Gaia

VOICES OF GAIA

ORACLE FOR PROSPERITY AND HARMONY ON EARTH

CHANNELED BY PATRICIA WALD-HOPKINS

The Oracle for Prosperity and Harmony on Earth is a channeled message as five separate Voices of Gaia transmissions: Mama Gaia, Mary Magdalene, The Holy Family, The Ruby Rose Lineage of The Immortality Stone, and Archangel Uriel. These five transmissions are woven together to create a five-dimensional message for humanity to receive at this time, to support their transition into their heart-centered lifestyles.

Voices of Gaia

My story of how I became an oracular channel called the Voices of Gaia—an oracle composed of many Voices that speak for the wisdom that is needed for these times of great change—began in 2015. At this time, I began speaking light language after being in a plant medicine ceremony. It took me a good three years before I could translate the light language codes I was speaking so quickly and passionately into written transmissions such as this, but I was able to create art and poem-like translations immediately. As a result, I became a prolific creator of digital art collages, and even created an oracle card deck, the *Infinite Self Oracle*.

My oracular channel name for Voices of Gaia is Aven Teija Greener. My birth name is Patricia Librada Gallegos and my married name is Patricia Librada Gallegos Wald-Hopkins, which are both sacred and beautiful, and also hold a vibration that carries ancestral distortions and obligations from my own biological family origins plus those of my husband's. These ancestral vibrations are not in true alignment with my soul essence vibrational frequency of the alignment of the stars on the day I was born. My incarnation frequency was distorted by the familial names that can only ever allow a certain aspect of my gifts to be used as an oracular channel.

My biggest challenge with being a channel has been around shame and self-doubt, which stemmed from the ancestral name lineage distortions and obligations, as well as the life experience that I created from those vibrations. When I left home after high school, I pursued degrees in biology and environmental health and toxicology. Western science became the backdrop for my life experience. It wasn't until I was thirty-five, about seventeen years ago and when I had a midlife crisis, that I began to explore the healing arts and my intuitive skills. And then, it took me a good while to trust my intuitive skills, and even longer to trust my oracular skills. I was overly concerned that I would say something "wrong," so I had to learn to become a clear and steady channel through much internal shadow work in the Akashic Records and with the Gene Keys, before I could hold the channel to be an oracle and have the transmissions be unfiltered by my ancestral heritage and life experiences. Note that I did not clear out all my ancestral heritage or life experiences, only those parts that distorted my ability to trust myself as a channel. The channel name, Aven Teija Greener, is a Kabalarian-balanced name and is my ceremonial name that allows me to step fully into a vibrationally clear and steady channel for Voices of Gaia.

What follows are five oracular transmissions from five different Voices of Gaia. A Voice of Gaia is a benevolent entity that wishes to share wisdom teaching for the highest good of the collective. At this time Mama Gaia, Mary Magdalene, The Holy Family, The Ruby Rose Lineage of The Immortality Stone, and Archangel Uriel wished to speak through me. These Voices are an integral part of my work as a Voices of Gaia Mentor to embody your unique Voice of Gaia using my New Earth Leadership Blueprint system, which is an initiatory journey for Voices of Gaia through eight archetype activation and embodiment portals . This is an initiatory journey of finding your heart-centered leadership Voice through the process of rooting into yourself and Mother Earth, opening to receive nourishment from the ecosystem of Gaia. And then—only then—from this place of ultimate stability, vitality, and integrity, aligning and fine tuning to your Voice of Gaia, your new earth leadership Voice, to foster prosperity and harmony on this beautiful planet we have chosen to inhabit as beings of light in human form.

Dimension 1: Message from Mama Gaia

What is your relationship with me, your Mother? Dear child who hides in the shadows of the trees, always following me yet never willing to show your beautiful face because, long ago, someone told you to hide in the darkness where you belong out of sight, never to be fully heard or seen in full light again. You are the Voice of Gaia. The Ancient One. The Childlike Wise One that whispers in the wind, and dances in the rain, and laughs and plays while the rest of the world toils and dies in sadness, for they have forgotten the sacred ways of life. You are the one who creates the fire in the hearts of those who hear and feel you, even though they do not see you, except as the beauty of Mama Gaia around them when they pause long enough to notice they are in a physical body that thrives when in communication with Me.

Why won't you speak up loud and clear, so they can stop dead in their tracks and turn around and truly see you for the first time? You live in each one of them. Let them behold your presence and grace as the keeper of the gate to Heaven on Earth. The keeper of the secrets of all dimensions of life on earth, for you are chosen as a Voice to speak for the creations of Gaia. You are the timeless timekeeper. The watcher of all the ways the world has been abused, as well as all the ways it has been honored, and celebrated, and cherished. You are the judge of the integrity of the ecosystem as we know it today. You must stop hiding in these times when your Voice will herald the navigation of the Great Change that is now upon us.

Most humans are lost and confused, and even those who think they know, and think they are on the enlightened path, are mistaken and fooled by their false pride. I know that when the trees begin to fall and we hear their cries as their roots die, and when the waves can no longer stop from washing the land bare because the ground is constantly shifting, they will still be surprised. This is not a time of saving the earth; Earth doesn't need saving. This is a time of celebrating our life, and all life, for the remaining time it can exist here on this planet. I want you to tell them to learn to listen again to the trees, and the rocks, and the spirits of life unseen. Stop the clock from ticking by being present in the moment to the beauty that is around you and will soon be gone as the earth is reborn again without *Homo sapiens*, using their flesh and bones as fertilizer for the New Earth where *Homo sanctus* and *Homo luminosa* call home. All this hustle and bustle to take care of the earth, yet we forget to enjoy just being present to Her. It is not that I do not appreciate you being mindful and cleaning up your messes now more than you used to, but you are missing the point of being alive. Cherish and celebrate the cornucopia of life, of my body and of yours.

We have gone over the tipping point. We are at the point of no return. We cannot go back to what was before. We can only enjoy the time we have here now and, yes, be mindful and be a good steward, but most importantly cultivate a relationship with Me. Talk to me. Hold me. Tell me your deepest desires and secrets because one day you will return in to Me. Let that time be a time where all that was hidden in guilt and shame has been brought to light and forgiven, so that the very essence of who you are, your soul, can be free while the elements of your body can be returned as the building blocks in the multiverse. I know people want to hear a brighter story—and perhaps some will instantaneously get on a spaceship or ascend into multidimensional space and avoid the chaos of the Great Change on Earth—but the end of the Earth as you humans know it, is upon us. Your existence has always been on the fast track to completion.

Life is precious and finite even though the soul is everlasting. There is no doubt that my own physical body will return to the Cosmic Womb. And what will become of my soul essence will reincarnate in another place, just as your soul essence will, so let yourselves find peace in these times instead of war. Create art and love. Eat well. Play. And stop working all the time. Stop building atrocities and making up stories about the value of such things. Stop wasting time trying to be rich and famous and just tell the Truth. You have to be the one to speak the Truth to them. You and the other Ancient Ones that have been in hiding must gather together now and set things straight about the importance of love. About living as the Lemurians once did in the 5D, before technology and greed took over and there was that Great Fall of Atlantis. We are on a repeat cycle and many know this. It is no secret that we have reached the pinnacle of our growth and are now in decline. So set out to bring magic to the world now, so that everyone's body may joyously sing the songs of Gaia, and celebrate the time we have left by loving one another in each moment and living each day in gratitude to the Source that gave you life in this physical body. You must return to the 5D consciousness to find this path to living in peace and pleasure in your physical body and with me at this time. Seek the teaching of those who have and continue to live in communion with Me, and be free to prosper and find harmony.

Dimension 2: Message from Mary Magdalene

Choose love. Choose only love, always and forever, in every moment. This is my prayer and blessing for you, my dear child, and for all the children. That they may return to love again, and again, and again. That they may never be sent to bed hungry, abandoned, and in an unnecessary circumstance of suffering for the lack of love. If I had one pearl of wisdom to offer you, dear child, to take out into the world right now—at this paramount and most precious moment—it would be a luminous pink pearl of the Divine Mother's Heart. And that this liquid, luminous, pearlescent pink orb of unconditional and undeniable love light frequency would infuse itself within you, and all around you, into the seen and unseen dimensions of your existence, and all existence. Like an elixir of healing balm for all the tender and wounded hearts of the children—the wounded inner child of each adult who walks in a trance of loneliness and abandonment, or in rage for the loss of innocence—the mass confusion that ensues when one has closed their heart to receive love.

I would have it that I could swaddle each broken heart in a blanket so soft and warm that it would want to open into the safety of this loving, motherly embrace. I want you, child, to tell the world in as loud a voice as you can—as a Voice of Gaia—that it is time to return to love. Love for self. Love for the innocent. Love for the lost. Love for the broken. Love for the angry. Love for the cruel hearted. Love for all of life. Love for Gaia. I am a priestess of the Red Rose of the Great Mother of the earth and the sacred plants from which the healing oils of my temples are made to anoint those in sickness and into death. These oils are also for alchemical transformation of those called into service of the Sacred Heart. Walk with me now, child, and be initiated as a bearer of the Sacred Heart. Bring the others to me now, before it is too late to open their hearts. The flowering of the heart is the last passage of humankind before the reckoning of all times falls upon us. Bring them all to stand witness to the luminous, pink, pearlescent light of undeniable Divine Love.

Let it dissolve their heart walls in an instantaneous moment of miraculous grace. Let the heart open so wide that they see the other side of the Universe within themselves and they know that they have returned to the Cosmic Womb, our Divine Mother, the Creator, the giver of all life. Let their divine essence be full and radiant once again. Let each return to innocence and their Divine Child blueprint. Return to the gardens of Eden again, and again, and again in this frequency of pink pearlescent and luminous light. From the temple of the Sacred Heart, let them gather once again to receive the manna from heaven to nourish and feed them in their lifetime on this glorious planet called Earth. Let them dance and sing again, celebrating joyously in celebration of all of life on Mama Gaia. This is my message I wish for you to share with the world, dear child, to live prosperously and harmoniously on earth.

Dimension 3: Message from the Holy Family

There is a brilliant light that shines within the heart of each child within a family. This is the light of the Divine Child within the human heart. It is the responsibility and the passion of the Divine Mother and the Divine Father to hold this precious heart with utmost and unending joyfulness and care. This way has been forgotten and superseded by a more base need to survive and to dominate those around us in order to feel secure and worthy of joy and, really, even just life.

There has been a great folly of the human spirit of losing touch with the value of Divine Life within the Heart of each one of us, that began as the struggle to survive the ordeals of childhood and goes back for generations and generations. We lost the way of the Holy

Family that is all about cultivating the Divine Light, the flame of Christas and Christos within the heart of each child that is born into the world. This Holy Family goes beyond the biological DNA that binds us to others. The Holy Family is the holy Tree of Life, and the purpose and passion as spiritually-aligned adults is to be the Divine Mother and Divine Father for every child that walks upon this Earth, to be fully present with them and bless them with great care and guidance with an open heart, so that they can grow into joyous adults that carry the lineage of joyful light into their lives and so on and so on.

There is a great sadness that fills the hearts of many at this time that is drowning the hope of the children to the point of them abandoning self-care and even sacred witness of the acts they do. It is a blindness to the depth of their soul presence and purpose in this lifetime that must be rekindled. It is most paramount to provide the space and the freedom to explore the depth of themselves without distraction by the need to survive. To support healthy nervous systems in our children is essential and critical to the New Earth consciousness that we, as the Holy Family, are here to foster through nourishing and supportive environments. We can no longer try one-size-fits-all or worse, look away, because it is across the world.

We must be present with the children with eyes wide open to the ripple effect across the globe, the solar system, the galaxy, the universe and beyond. We must share with them the ways of love, and only love, for without this foundation of unconditional love, we seek success in ways that deplete rather than complete us. We seek for only the material without it being deeply rooted in the spiritual. We end up seeking work for the pay rather than for the satisfaction. We seek things to comfort us rather than going within to know that all we need is within us, and all we need on the physical plane is what nourishes us and allows us to grow in love and in community. The age of the lone wolf has ended. The return home to the Tree of Life is upon us, so heed these words and root back into love in all ways as we raise the children of the New Earth in prosperity and harmony.

Dimension 4: Message from the Ruby Rose Lineage of the Immortality Stone

In order to gain access to the immortality stone, you must become an initiate of the Ruby Rose Lineage of 5D New Earth consciousness. In order to become an initiate, you must travel the path of the open heart. You must become the Lover to all. The immortality stone is the ruby as red as the beautiful rose of Sara.

Sara is the Goddess of Love in the temples of Love in the 5D. She is a heart-based being that has seen many incarnations of human form fractals in the earth's existence. She is mainly embodied in all Beauty in the world, like the red roses one gives a Lover that represent life force and vitality—the one pure, beating heart. This is the kundalini life force we speak of here and the bearers of this lineage all wear white or scarlet red robes. They wear the immortality stone upon their neck, which allows them to be in human form through all time and space and dimensions, and to help those who have been broken and want to love again, to walk the road of the red rose of the open heart of the temples of Sara in the 5D.

This is the path of the beloved, not of the human love on Valentine's Day, but the path back to the Divine Beloved Nature of Love that is within the One Heart of God and is directly connected to the 5D—allowing one to exist in immortality once the 3D plane begins to collapse. It is the path of the *bodhisattva*—a path for those who are willing to be left behind and forgo ascension for a time to help the others onto the red rose path of the open heart of the beloved resurrection into the great Halls of Amenti. Begin this path by contemplating the frequency of the ruby ray light of the royal line of Lyran on the star of Vega. Seek the support of astrology to align with this path of Love and Devotion. Wear a ruby upon your neck as a reminder of how important Love is to prosperity and harmony on this earth plane, and to access the 5D heart plane for sanctuary during this time of Great Change.

Dimension 5: Message from Archangel Uriel

A blessing for prosperity and harmony on Earth.

Lay your holy body upon the warm earth and let the golden rays of the sun shine upon you and through you, illuminating each cell in your body and each strand of DNA. Let this golden light activate the codes of prosperity, the twelve-stranded DNA, that are your birthright in this very lifetime. Feel the warmth of the sun rush through your body, awakening the golden god/ goddess within you. You now hold the frequency of resplendent earth. The earth that is so alive and fertile with organic life that nourishes itself in symbiotic ecosystems. Your body itself has now become its own symbiotic ecosystem, continually feeding upon the regenerative golden light that is now continually emanating from your DNA and is continually active in your cells.

As you lay upon the warm earth, your golden light-activated cells begin to communicate with the microbes, and the crystals, and the minerals. You see you are now a direct conduit of the golden light codes of prosperity—directly from your cells into all biotic and abiotic forms on earth. You are the blessing of this new age of *being with* Mother Nature rather than *doing to* Her.

When you can find the stillness and repose to rest and gather the golden light of the sun into your body, you become the blessing of life force the planet needs to be regenerated for many generations to come—until you all have found your way into your light bodies and are called home to the stars from which you came, and from the Cosmic Womb from which your very soul was born. Be that blessing for your planet now, and take the time to commune with Her in stillness and reverence; this is how you will tap into the prosperity in your lifetime that is your birthright and that will create a field of nourishment for you and for all. It truly is that simple.

And do not be fooled by the clouds and the rain that cover the sun, or the clothing upon your skin, for the sun is still shining and, until it stops, this source of prosperity is available to you even in the darkest of times. When you partake and share Light in communion with the Gaia, you create harmony on Earth. Life comes into balance. Equilibrium is continually met despite the turbulence. And do not be afraid of death, for in death there is rebirth and you will all go through so many mini-deaths and rebirths in the coming years that you will truly understand the beautiful life of the butterfly. You will truly come to understand the meaning of life and death, and that there is balance in all things, and from this place prosperity and harmony are found on Earth.

Closing Prayer

The only way through the Great Change is as a fully embodied Heart Being. With the heartbeat of Mama Gaia and the love of the angels, may you find the way deep into your Sacred Heart, and unlock the door, and open to the blessed field of unconditional love, forgiveness, and acceptance that we all may walk hand-in-hand home to unite with the One Heart of all that is. This is the joyful path to the prosperity and harmony of New Earth.

ABOUT THE AUTHOR

Patricia Wald-Hopkins is a Voice of Gaia, Modern Mystic, Infinite Self Catalyst, and Soul Liberation Guide for those ready to break free from old paradigm limitations, awaken to their Infinite Self, and lead the life they are DIVINELY designed to live as a Voice of Gaia.

As an Akashic Records Wisdom Guide, creator of the Butterfly Healing Method™, Gene Keys Ambassador and Guide, and co-founder of the School of Light Collective, she supports her clients to fully embody their Infinite Self and Voice of Gaia.

An author in several best selling collaborative books, Patricia's chapters include: 'The Miracle of Light Language: Awakening to My Soul Voice and Purpose' in the book, *Miraculous*; 'Butterfly Medicine Healing' in *Energy Healing & Soul Medicine*; 'Stardust Blood: Codes for Harmony on Earth' in *Awakening Starseeds: Dreaming Into The Future, Volume 3*, and 'Anointing Oils of the Goddess' in *Stories of the Goddess: Divine Feminine Frequency Keepers*. She is also the creator of the Infinite Self Oracle Card deck and creator and host of the Divinely Inspired Woman podcast.

- Podcast: https://podcasts.apple.com/us/podcast/the-divinely-inspired-woman-podcast/id1662728359
- Website: www.Patriciawaldhopkins.com

Your Life is a Garden

THE GARDEN OF EDEN

CHANNELED BY JESSICA ROSALIE

*B*eloved Child of God,

Today I invite you to come on a sacred journey with me. For many of you, this place feels like home. This home I speak of is known as The Garden of Eden. For this journey, all that is required is for you to open your heart. I invite you now to place a hand on your heart and surrender to the divine flow of your rhythmic heartbeat. Allow your senses to guide you and feel all of your worries, concerns, doubts, and fears wash away. *Breathe deeply* and let go completely.

If, at any point along this journey, you feel yourself drifting into your mind, I invite you to repeat this mantra:

I AM the beauty of God, within and throughout every aspect of my being. I am whole. I am love.

Before we begin, let us start by setting a few intentions.

Beloved God, Holy Mother, Holy Father, the Divine I AM Presence and Source Within,

I pray for all those who are ready to return home to their hearts to be blanketed in the love of Source while reading these words.

May every word reflect back to you your own innate wisdom, Source connection, and remembrance of how truly special and loved you really are.

May this chapter bring you closer to God within you, so that you may continue to be a beacon of truth, unconditional love, and a pillar for those in your life who need the reminder of who they truly are.

I pray that we all find the courage within ourselves to share our gifts with the world and allow our light to shine through our creations as we remember: *We are the beauty of God.*

So it is. So it is. It is done.

Let us now settle into this space. Allow your thoughts to drift, your mind to rest, and allow the frequency of peace to wash over you. With every breath out, feel your body begin to soften as you telepathically let your body know it is safe to relax and you are open to receive for your highest good today.

Imagine, now, your heart as a beautiful rose. Witness this rose as it blossoms within you and admire the beauty that is your sacred heart flower. With intention, see this rose opening its petals. Feel the sensation of what it feels like to truly open your heart without fear or limitation. When our heart is open, we allow Source light to flow through us like a stream or flow of pure Omni love. Remember this is your true nature. Let go of all resistance, all need to understand, all need to try to do anything, and just be.

Continue to breathe in love from your heart space and breathe out love, witnessing the expansion and connection to God within you.

Mantra: *I AM the beauty of God, within and throughout every aspect of my being. I am whole. I am love.*

Now, Beloved, within your heart, see a golden door begin to appear; it emanates the light of Source so bright it looks like pure gold. This door will take you to the sacred Garden of Eden—a place of pure Omni Love. When you are ready, see yourself opening this door and walking through the portal of your sacred rose heart.

Continue to breathe, slowly and deeply. I invite you to take three deep breaths. With every breath in and out, feel your frequency begin to rise. Now feel the opening of your channels to receive the liquid plasma, living, breathing light of Source filling your vessel.

In your mind's eye, see the opalescent and pearlescent hues around you beginning to take form as the most magnificent, sparkling garden you have ever seen. The flowers in this garden are the creation of pure Omni Love. Each flower in this garden is a unique creation. Not one flower is like the other as each holds its own unique beauty, grace, and light. Together these living, breathing, radiant flowers make up the beauty of creation itself.

You notice that the air around you, with each breath, fills your lungs with pure, rainbow, plasma light. Every molecule, every plant, every elemental, and every animal you meet in this garden is the living, breathing, organic lifeforce of God. Allow yourself to be nurtured here. Truly embrace the experience, remembering that everything you see, everything you feel, and everything you touch is a reflection of the beauty of your own light, your own essence, and your own soul.

Mantra: *I AM the beauty of God, within and throughout every aspect of my being. I am whole. I am love.*

Notice how enhanced your senses are here. Breathe in the pure love fragrance of the roses, lilacs, and peonies. Feel the softness of every blade of grass brushing your bare feet with every step. Admire the dancing of colour and light around you as you see pearlescent hues of aquamarine, magenta pink, golden yellows, emerald greens, and violet rays taking form. Tune into the sounds of flowing streams, rustling leaves, and the flourishing of life creating a symphony of songs around you.

Now focus your awareness on the songs of creation. As you focus, you begin to hear music. The gardens are singing to you. Each flower is vibrating at its own unique frequency of sound and emanating pure beauty and love in the form of songs. These songs are connecting with your own heart flower, and you notice that your heart is beginning to join in and sing its own, unique, heart song. Feel the harmonising frequencies activate a remembrance of your own soul song. This song within you is as ancient as the birthing of your unique soul light. In this moment you are remembering that, just like the flowers in the Gardens of Eden, you too are made up of colour, light, and sound. You, too, represent the beauty of God within and throughout. You ARE the purity of love consciousness. You ARE God experiencing itself in human form.

Do you remember now where you came from?

Do you remember now the power that you hold?

Do you remember now the beauty, grace, and love that you truly are and always have been?

Beloved Child, Source has never left you. You were never abandoned. You were never lost. You were never left behind, forgotten, or deemed unworthy.

God has always been with you because *you are God*. You cannot lose that which you already are, you can only forget. But now it is time, Dear One, to remember.

Mantra: *I AM the beauty of God, within and throughout every aspect of my being. I am whole. I am love.*

The Garden of Eden is a reflection of your own soul. You have created this space today through the beauty of your own heart, your own soul, and your own light. Everything that you see, feel, touch, and smell is a representation of the love that you are. This is how creations are made—through our remembrance that Source is a living, breathing, stream of consciousness that has the ability to take form in any way that it chooses. This is why we are all one. This is why separation and division is only an illusion. This is why fear is not real, not truly. God is Omni Love. Anything that is not love, is not God. Anything that is not God, is not who you truly are. You may experience fear, separation, pain, or suffering, but you must remember that, at any time, you can choose to return to your true, core, soul essence which is, and always will be, love. This is your true home. This is your true nature as an angelic human.

The journey of the soul is one that has many lessons and experiences for us. Through our many incarnations, we have many opportunities to *try on experiences* that our soul chooses. Through these experiences, we begin to shape our consciousness. We are the accumulation of all of our lived experiences throughout time and space, past, present, and future. Just like our human life has shaped and guided us to become who we are today, our many lifetimes and experiences have influenced and formed the uniqueness of our own soul.

Do you see *now* how truly special you are? Not one aspect of creation is like the other. You are as unique as your fingerprint, the way you laugh, and the sound of your voice.

God does not judge you, or think any less of you, based on your experiences. How could Source judge itself for having an experience when this is what we are created to do? In fact, the reality is, you being here now took a tremendous amount of courage. Do you remember being chosen to be here now to help guide our family home?

Children of the Light – The Awakened Starseed: New Earth Mission

We are in the age of remembering. The dawn of a new era of change; one that will bring harmony, peace, and freedom to our planet and its inhabitants.

Right now, we are experiencing a global shift in consciousness. All over the world, people are beginning to ask questions and open their hearts to the truth that resides within them. We are the Seekers, the Pathfinders, the Wayshowers, and the Dreamweavers who have come to help humanity reach its full potential as a human race.

Each one of you holds the very key needed to unlock and decode your own reality. It is important to understand that awakening is not only for those who are special; we are all beautiful and unique in our own expression. Awakening is a choice that we wanted to experience, and a calling from deep within us to remember the wholeness of who we are. It is a natural part of our evolution as a soul—and it is a gift.

In every moment we must choose our highest conscious path. We are here to show a new way to exist, one that is built on the foundations of freedom, unconditional love, and unity. Humanity is ready for this great change. As a collective, we have chosen to heal our past so that we can bring about a better and brighter future for all of humanity. We must allow ourselves to be free from that which confines us, that which dims our light, and that which suppresses our very nature. We will no longer believe the stories that tell us that we are broken, that we are not enough, and that this is just the way things are and always have been.

We did not come here to blend in. We did not come here to compromise, or to create more of the same. No, we came here to rise. We came here to be our most radiant and beautiful selves. We will no longer dim our lights because we shine too brightly. Our light is one that can no longer be hidden. As more and more of us wake up, our

Earth is ascending. Mother Gaia is celebrating us, congratulating us on our bravery, and letting us know that we can achieve the impossible. Humanity is remembering their divinity, their love, and their light. It is a beautiful time to be alive, as this is a time of celebration and a time to create.

The New Earth will be built through the creation of our conscious thoughts, emotions, and actions. Many of you may ask how you can even begin to create such profound shifts and changes on the planet, as it may feel like no easy feat. I am here to remind each one of you that every time you choose love over fear, and unity over separation, you are creating New Earth. Every time you choose to hold your pillar of light in full, and allow your consciousness to shine through your heart, you are creating New Earth. Every day that you wake up and ask yourself, "How can I be of full service to humanity and choose my highest conscious path?" you are creating New Earth. Every time you choose to love yourself through all the tears, through all the heartache, and you tell yourself that you are worthy, you are creating New Earth. You see, *we* are New Earth. We are creating New Earth *through* us. New Earth is not outside of us. New Earth is not a destination or a faraway land. New Earth is inside of each one of you. We are New Earth rising as one. Each of you holds a piece of New Earth through your own unique expression of your consciousness; this is where our true power and potential lies. When we can remember that we are sovereign creators, then we can—and will—achieve anything far greater than our self-imposed limitations.

The questions we need to ask ourselves are:

Are we ready?

Are we ready and willing to let go of everything that we may think we know, and allow ourselves to feel the truth that wants to be experienced through the portal of our own hearts?

Can we release anything and everything that is holding us back from revealing who we truly are?

Can we love ourselves so deeply, intimately, and authentically that all deeply-rooted traumas are healed through the loving embrace and space we hold for ourselves?

Can we choose to love all of ourselves, our experiences, and the wisdom we have gained through them, so we can open up to our unlimited potential?

Are we ready to ignite our God Spark and make room for our higher consciousness to be anchored through us?

Are we ready to show up for ourselves each and every day, knowing that this journey will push us to be our greatest selves in every way?

This journey will ask us to be seen, to be heard, and to feel and release all that is not us, so we can embody all we came here to be.

It is a path for those who are no longer willing to compromise who they are, and it is a journey that will require us to stand in our Truth. We will be tested, and we will have to let go of what is not aligned to make room for the New World we are creating. It is, however, a path of the highest honour; one that will offer you true freedom, happiness, and complete unconditional love.

The universe has chosen you. It was not a mistake, as you would not be here right now if you were not ready. You must, however, choose it for yourself—now or later, it is your decision. You are fully supported and loved, always.

We Are Remembering

In order to remember who we are, we must first remind ourselves of who we are not. We are not the stories we tell ourselves, we are not our emotions, and we are not definitely not our mind, or our thoughts. We simply are, and that is enough. In that state of "just being," we understand that we are everything and nothing at the same time. We must acknowledge that who we are is not one thing, or even a list of things, as we are infinite beings of light having a human experience. Each one of you is as vast and as magnificent as the universe. Your consciousness is limitless and ever-expanding.

Many of us have lived most of our lives experiencing everything as set, defined, and labelled. We have identified as our jobs, our titles, our degrees, and our accomplishments. We are attached to these identities as if we would be lost without them. We have held onto experiences, people, and situations even when we knew they were not good for us, because it was what we knew; it was safe and familiar.

The journey of awakening is much like being an actor on a stage who suddenly becomes aware of the audience. The veil is lifted and we begin to understand that we are not defined by the roles we are playing; who we really are is so much more than what we see on stage. We begin to see that the people in our life are also just playing their roles, the experiences we are having are just one version of reality, and we remember that we can choose a new story whenever we are ready. We begin to remember that we are the director of our own play, and that we can choose to re-write or change the script at any time.

It is through our own awakening that we begin to see our lives from a much wider, more "zoomed-out" perspective. It is through this expansion that we allow ourselves to become the creators of our own lives. In this expanded state, we are able to become the observer, and from this new, heightened perspective, suddenly the maze of our own life and the interwoven streams of light that make up our reality become much clearer to us. We no longer feel confined, limited, or trapped by our own mind illusions. We begin to perceive life differently; it's more beautiful and magical. In this moment, we know that we did not come here to be ordinary. We realise that we have been given the opportunity to truly become the artists of our own lives. It is through this shift that we begin to allow our own essence, our consciousness, and God Spark to be reborn.

Affirmations for Conscious Expansion and Awareness

I am not my mind, experiences, or emotions; I am the awareness behind them.

I have the ability to choose my reality through my thoughts and my reactions.

I allow myself to expand my consciousness and raise my frequency by bringing awareness to each moment.

I let go of all attachments to outcomes, identities, and stories so that I may allow my higher self to step forward and lead.

I consciously choose to become aware of when I need to allow and when I need to release control when I am holding on too tightly.

I hold inside of me the very key to my own heart, and through unlocking this connection to myself, I unleash the wisdom, power, and freedom of my own soul.

You Did Not Come Here To Follow

You did not come here to follow. Each one of you holds the spirit of a warrior inside you. Each one of you carries a light that can be seen from far above the cosmos. It is not by chance that you are here, now, in this moment, reading these words. If you have found this book, then you know that you came to Earth with a mission and a purpose that is far greater than you can possibly imagine. You feel a knowingness inside you, in your heart, that great change is upon us and that you were chosen to be a part of this great change.

We have been called many names over time: Starseeds, Lightworkers, Rainbow Warriors, the 144,000, the Volunteers, The Ground Crew, and so on. These names are not overly important as they tend to try to define and categorise something that is undefinable. These names, however, remind each one of us that we belong to a group of souls who chose to be here, right now, to assist in raising the collective consciousness of the planet, to help the Earth ascend, and to guide humanity as we usher in the Golden Age.

Beloved,
You are unfolding.
The universe is all wrapped up inside your perfect human vessel.
But alas, it is time to witness the greatness that is inside.
You mustn't be afraid of your divine gifts and beauty, for what you have to share is much needed in the world at this time.
Be prepared, Dear One, for beyond the horizon not too far away, there is a grand destiny that awaits you.
A destiny and mission that you will not miss and cannot fail for all of your ancestors, the beautiful and wise men and women who came before you, are walking alongside you with a fierce powerful wind that cannot be tamed.
You have the elements of fire, water, earth, air, and aether on your side.
You have the grandness of the universe and the star nations shining their light upon you and illuminating your path every step of the way.
Know that inside yourself, you hold the key to unlocking the most important masterpiece that there is.
Your existence is that of love—and what a precious gift you are.
Thank you, beautiful soul, for being here.
Thank you, darling angel of light, for spreading your wings and taking on this grand opportunity to show the world all that you are.
You mustn't hide now for the world needs your light.
Shine,
My darling,
SHINE
In love and grace,
Jessica Rosalie

ABOUT THE AUTHOR

Jessica Rosalie is an oracle, teacher, empathic healer, and energetic channel offering transmissions of pure love.

In the Spring of 2019, she underwent a profound spiritual awakening, experiencing a transformative shift that realigned her with her true soul purpose. She then began to develop her intuitive and empathic gifts to teach and guide others in connecting more deeply with their true heart and soul expression.

Writing has always served as Jessica's sanctuary for self-expression, offering her solace and profound healing. In 2019, she began to publicly share her poems and creations. In doing so, she realized that what she felt and experienced, so many others could relate to—and it brought them deep comfort, and healing. Her dream to be a published author, so her words could reach the hearts of others, has now been realized.

During the year-long journey of writing, editing, and preparing for the release of her chapter in the book, *Oracle,* Jessica went through another transformational healing and heart expansion. Through this rebirth, *The Garden of Eden* has now energetically taken form as an online portal. Eden is a sanctuary for those who are looking to receive the transmissions of divine love, nourishment, and peace to support them in their daily life.

You can now enroll in *The Garden of Eden* through the link below.
https://jessicarosalie.thinkific.com/courses/eden

Connect with Jessica Rosalie:
Email: jessica.rainbowgoddess@gmail.com
Website: www.therainbowgoddess.com
Youtube: The Rainbow Goddess
Instagram: @the.rainbowgoddess
Facebook: Jessica Rosalie
LinkTree: linktr.ee/therainbowgoddess

You Are Pefect And Pure

YOU ARE PERFECT AND PURE

CHANNELED BY CYNTHIA PORTLOCK

My dear child. If only I could get you to see yourself in the same way that I see you. You are already perfect. You are already whole. You are loved and protected far more than you can comprehend. Trust this. Let the vibration of these words ring through your being, awakening you now to your divinity. Even amongst the chaos and confusion around you, there is nothing that you need to change or fix. Only allow.

Right NOW, without changing anything about yourself, KNOW that you are PERFECT. Not who you think you are. Not who you are becoming. You-right-NOW, exactly as you are in this very moment.

In this knowing, allow all expectations and judgments of yourself to gently fall away. You have been too hard on yourself for far too long. Surrender into this endless embrace of divine mother's love. Allow your heart to unfurl so it can receive the nourishment and light that will feed your soul, that you may never hunger or thirst again. Remember that you are the beloved child of the most high, created in their likeness and image. There are no mistakes.

YOU ARE PERFECT AND PURE

I see the purity of your sacred heart. I see your innocence. I see your indestructible soul, and your relentless spirit. See yourself with my eyes, for we are ONE.

It is through the purity of your sacred heart that you can command miracles. It is through your innocence that holds your power to both create and destroy. Embrace both, for together exists a sacred loop of unlimited potential. One can not exist without the other.

It is through this continuous cycle of creation and destruction that you can continuously explore, experiment, and expand. This is not something to fear. Rather, this is something to joyfully celebrate. Allow your Phoenix Child to RISE, and playfully use this power from within you to test the boundaries of what you thought was possible. Discover your endless creative potential. For YOU rising in your power and authenticity IS the gift of grace surrounding Mother Earth now. You are a chosen ONE.

Release all fears around destruction and decay now. For you already know that nothing is ever wasted. Allow yourself to receive nourishment from this natural process by not resisting or clinging on. Gift yourself with time and space and explore the depths of your soul. When grief arises, know that each tear is crystalizing your love from within. The fall of each tear creates a tantric union with your Beloved Mother Earth, an offering to Her that is healing Her from the core, and therefore healing the land on which you walk. Walk gently and feel Her love and gratitude fueling you in this symbiotic embrace, in the most magical and miraculous ways.

With an open heart, use your voice as a powerful instrument of truth, light, love, and wisdom. Create your deepest desires with the power of your words. Like a high-pitch shrill can shatter glass, use your voice to shatter the illusions that attempt to choke the growth of New Earth. Both are essential to create balance and harmony

Teach by example. Love freely. Surrender to awe and wonder. Behold, the promised land has awakened.

I love you, Isis, Auset, Divine Mother

Channeled by Cynthia Portlock, Voice of Gaia

ABOUT THE AUTHOR

Cynthia Portlock is a navigator of the unseen worlds devoted to anchoring love and wisdom for Sophia Gaia's ascension. Utilizing gifts as an Ordained Magdalene Priestess, Akashic Wisdom Keeper, Shamanic Practitioner, and Certified Sophia Circle Leader™, she supports your Higher Self Embodiment as you step into your authentic leadership.

A Lover of the diversity of *all life* in *all forms*, Cynthia guides you into remembrance of who you are with an open mind and curious heart. She specializes in ancestral healing, guided energy medicine, Akashic readings/clearings, and the creation of containers that support your expansion and transformation.

Cynthia loves, sees, and accepts you as you are, exactly where you are; never too little or too much. She warmly welcomes you in your ecstatic bliss *and* your rage or grief.

Email: Cynthia@mothergaiasgarden.com
You Tube: @mothergaiasgarden870
Website: www.sophiasdragonsden.com

MOON GODDESS PUBLISHING

Moon Goddess Publishing is a beacon for Divine feminine leaders, Wayshowers, and Visionaries on a mission to uplift humanity. Our goal is to amplify their voices and create a profound impact during this time of ascension. Through publishing books of light, we seek to empower, inspire, and activate change.

Fueled by a deep love for books and their transformative power, we strive to establish a publishing company that reaches the masses, builds community, and fosters collaboration. We believe in the collective strength of purpose and aim to leave a positive imprint on the world, so creating a legacy for future generations.

At Moon Goddess Publishing, we hold to the values of Authenticity, Truth, Collaboration, Leadership, Service to humanity, Empowerment, Joy, and the Divine feminine essence in all forms. These values guide us in everything we do, as we strive to make a lasting impact that will resonate for generations to come.

If you're prepared to share your unique story and begin a

transformative journey of self-discovery and empowerment, Abigail warmly invites you to explore the possibilities for collaboration with Moon Goddess Publishing, or to engage in her exclusive programs: Elevated Empath and Goddess Unleashed.

Website: www.moongoddessacademy.com
Facebook: https://www.facebook.com/abigail.mensahbonsu.7/
Facebook group: https://www.facebook.com/groups/MoonGoddessSanctum
Podcast:https://podcasters.spotify.com/pod/show/sovereigngoddess
Instagram: https://www.instagram.com/moongoddessmentor/

Made in United States
Orlando, FL
13 June 2024